LEADERSHIP
FOR
COMPETITIVE ADVANTAGE

LEADERSHIP
FOR
COMPETITIVE ADVANTAGE

Nick Georgiades
and
Richard Macdonell

JOHN WILEY & SONS
Chichester • New York • Weinheim • Brisbane • Singapore • Toronto

Other Wiley Editorial Offices

John Wiley & Sons, Inc., 605 Third Avenue,
New York, NY 10158-0012, USA

WILEY-VCH Verlag GmbH, Pappelallee 3,
D-69469 Weinheim, Germany

Jacaranda Wiley Ltd, 33 Park Road, Milton,
Queensland 4064, Australia

John Wiley & Sons (Asia) Pte Ltd, 2 Clementi Loop #02-01,
Jin Xing Distripark, Singapore 129809

John Wiley & Sons (Canada) Ltd, 22 Worcester Road,
Rexdale, Ontario M9W 1L1, Canada

Library of Congress Cataloging-in-Publication Data
Georgiades, Nick
    Leadership for competitive advantage/by Nick Georgiades & Richard Macdonell.
        p.   cm.
    Includes bibliographical references and index.
    ISBN 0-471-97928-7 (acid-free paper)
    1. Leadership.   2. Management.   I. Macdonell, Richard.
    II. Title.
    HD57.7.G46   1998
    658.4'092—dc21
                                                    97-31196
                                                    CIP

British Library Cataloguing in Publication Data
A catalogue record for this book is available from the British Library

ISBN 0-471-97928-7

Typeset in 11/13pt Garamond from the author's disks by
Footnote Graphics, Warminster, Wiltshire
Printed and bound in Great Britain by Bookcraft (Bath) Ltd, Midsomer Norton, Somerset
This book is printed on acid-free paper responsibly manufactured from sustainable forestry, in which at least two trees are planted for each one used for paper production.

CONTENTS

FOREWORD

In a strange sort of way, the former British Prime Minister, John Major, has reason to be grateful that this book was published after his term of office ended.

Had it not been – and had he read it – there would have been little need for him to inquire famously: 'What is this vision thing?' As it is, John Major's immortality, in those books of famous quotations and sayings, is most probably assured.

In *Leadership For Competitive Advantage*, Nick Georgiades and Richard Macdonell explain how vision is the elusive ingredient which added in equal quantity to strong leadership, creates success.

But this is no purely academic treatise speaking from the safe surroundings of the business school lecture room. Its messages come laced with the authentic grit of experience from the working board room, the factory floor and the competitive marketplace.

One of the authors worked alongside me in one of the toughest business assignments I have ever faced – the transformation of British Airways from a disliked and dysfunctional state-owned corporation, into arguably the most successful international airline in the world.

The book draws from such experience to create a path of light and logic through the most difficult of business territories – the territory of change. It brings home that most simple, yet oft-neglected, truth that the only meaningful job of a manager is the management of change.

Through these pages and chapters comes the lesson that real long-term business stimulus must be identified and separated from the distractions of short-term style. Importantly, a model is created to help the reader through this conundrum, although the book is not so pretentious as to believe it has every answer.

I hear echoes of our experience at British Airways in the argument which proposes the need for a 'Driving Alliance', that is a pan-company dedication to change which has, as its chief characteristic, a commitment to break down barriers of hierarchy and practice. Such alliance can only be achieved, however, if every individual concerned understands the reasons for change and is shown the precise objectives and the way of achieving them.

Argument over whether leadership and management are the same or different has long held sway in the seminar rooms and continues to do so. This book raises the level of that debate by placing it in an organisation-wide context. The authors maintain careful balance between the academic and the pragmatic, but with obvious passion for the need to do something to bring the human element back into the world of work, never mind the field of Human Resource Management.

The book holds true to what I have always believed which is that the job of a leader is to weld disparate groups of people together as one team, able and determined to achieve exceptional results for their customers, their shareholders and for each other.

This proposition is analysed and broken down and presented in four key elements: facing the uncertainties in an external environment; creating vision for change; developing an adaptive, flexible culture; and specifying precisely which management practices are necessary.

I commend *Leadership For Competitive Advantage* to all those who aspire to build lasting business success.

Sir Colin Marshall
Chairman, British Airways
President, Confederation of British Industry

PREFACE AND ACKNOWLEDGEMENTS

This book has grown out of our joint experience as both 'thinkers and doers'. We hope to be able to make the links between some management ideas that have not previously been knitted together in the fields of corporate strategy, human resource strategy and marketing. They have been some time in preparation and have developed, in practical terms, from a variety of leadership development activities.

The earliest of these was the UK version of a programme developed by the Center for Creative Leadership in North Carolina and in subsequent variations for the World Bank and British Airways. The British Airways programme was known as *Managing People First* and represented the essential core of the wide-ranging culture change programme carried out between 1984 and 1989 while Nick Georgiades was Director of Human Resources at British Airways.

The book is not just about British Airways although it makes clear, for the first time, some of the underlying philosophies that drove the change process there between 1983 and 1989. The need for a dedicated group of people to take the change process forward has led us to postulate the need for what we call a *driving alliance*. In the years since 1989, initial ideas have been refined into a training programme often called *Leadership for Competitive Advantage* which has been delivered to more than 500 managers and leaders. We dedicate this book to all of these 'dreamers of the day' who have been brave enough to take our amalgam of conceptual ideas and practical advice and attempted to use both to put some humanness and benevolence back into their business perspectives.

We have seen over the years the four imperatives of the leader's role being acted out before our eyes. The need to cope with a changing external environment, to create a vision for change, to build an adaptive culture and to specify clearly what is expected of managers, has been modelled by many significant leaders who have helped shape our thinking and whom we gratefully acknowledge here. They are Sir Colin Marshall, Roger Bellis, Jean Carr, Kenneth Gilbert, Adrian Hosford, Sue Hunt, Michael Levin, Martin Reynolds, Simon Stone, Ken Vowles, Les Wilkinson and Barry Woledge. Their influence and stimulus have kept us constantly alert to the often contradictory needs of organisational leadership.

We have been influenced too by our interactions with some significant thinkers and writers in our own discipline. We acknowledge our debt to their genius and insights. They are Warren Bennis, Warner Burke, Gerard Egan, George Litwin, Morgan McCall, Lynda Phillimore and Michael Zuckerman. We particularly acknowledge Fernand Vaquer as a continual source of inspiration. We have tried to translate their ideas into action and offer them our first apologies if somewhere along the line we have failed.

Our debt to our colleagues in NGA and Salford University is profound. Jan Chalmers, Janet Brown and Cliff West helped us in ways too numerous to mention and most of all to Daphne Georgiades who showed us what leadership was really about.

Chapter One
FIRST THINGS FIRST

AN INTRODUCTION TO TRANSFORMATION

This is a book about making businesses better. Better for shareholders. Better for customers and better (much better) for employees.

For 60 years or so we have worked in, observed, studied and have been customers of hundreds of different organisations. That accumulated experience has driven us to search for the answer to one simple question. Why do we find organisations (both public and private sector), so full of intelligent people, working for so many hours, with so little apparent joy and with so little apparent success? In short, why does work have to be so joyless for so many and why are enterprises apparently so unable to deliver the goods?

As customers of enterprise we still gasp at the way our banks treat us as servile recipients of their current direct marketing campaigns; at the way surly, disengaged cabin-crew do us the honour of allowing us to mess up their antimacassars, while preening and giggling amongst themselves; at the way our garage convinced us that a new 'stub-axle' would cure the steering problem for £200 but without a sign of contrition or explanation when it does not; at the way we are consistently lied to about the availability of products in a mail-order catalogue; at hotels who deny to callers that we are registered there, deliver mangled messages or fail to deliver at all; at the unavailability of anyone to take ownership of issues in our dealings with local government, at the response *nobody else has complained*. And on and on! A weekly, monthly catalogue of individual experiences that defies comprehension. Surely these businesses have heard of customer service training or TQM or something! Don't they know that the Customer is King! Yet?

As employees we have been the victims of an uncomprehending manager who refused to allow us time off to greet the arrival of our first-born; the manager who demanded incessant attention to minute details on a particular project, but who did nothing himself to ensure its success, and then took the credit; the lies and deceits that permanently occupied the gossip of ourselves and our colleagues; the hours of fruitless conjecture about *them upstairs and what they are up to* and the impact it would have upon us, our sanity, our egos and our livelihoods.

We have been bamboozled by organisational memoranda which compelled timely action but whose meaning and purpose were veiled in incomprehensible clouds of mystery or jargon (usually from the Personnel Department). We have been demoralised by the boss's secretary who demanded attendance *forthwith* at an unscheduled meeting, but who was unwilling to give an insight into the subject. We have been deflated by the team leader's instruction to contribute with the words: *And now for the comedy turn!* Had none of these folks done Supervision 101? Had not their MBA tutors asked for an essay on Leadership? Had they not heard of the *One Minute Manager*?

As academics and consultants we shudder at the incidents we have encountered of the use of unbridled power in the suppression of individual workers (*I can't talk to you about that because I'll get the sack!*) and observed dysfunctional hierarchies created simply to ensure sufficient distribution of job-evaluation points.

We have led training events, endorsed and exhorted by senior managers, who disdainfully and wilfully acted in exact contradiction of the training's key messages (*I did not get where I am today by . . .*). We have at other times counselled individual employees who have been psychologically discarded but who continue to be employed, because no one had the courage to manage with care their graceful and dignified egress.

We have learned of the drunk in senior management about whom the advice is offered *Try and see her before lunch*; and of the marketing department headed by an individual whose intellectual ability precluded any possibility of understanding the market research statistics, let alone brand segmentation; or the CEO whose sole *raison d'être* was to secure his knighthood and whose perception of his role was dominated entirely by that need. We have frequently stimulated the exasperation of so many senior folk who willingly and with commitment attended to the enterprise and its mission but who were aghast at the suggestion that their role demanded more than simply satisfying the needs of the shareholders.

All of this frustration and astonishment accumulates towards the end of professional careers in which we have seen, or even been involved in campaigns for national organisation renewal. We were involved in preaching the virtues of the Industrial Training Act 1974; one of us worked, albeit briefly, at the Work Research Unit of the Department of Employment, where a free advisory service for the redesign of work was on offer.

We watched and applauded Commissions that noted the value of greater industrial democracy. More recently Total Quality Management, BS 5750, Investors in People, competency statements for national qualification in management and, latterly, business re-engineering all have been hailed as the ultimate panacea for the demise or revitalisation of British commerce and industry.

In addition, British management has not been isolated from the waves of enthusiasm that start on the other side of the Atlantic Ocean. First, T-groups and the Human Relations school. Starting as that movement did under the influence of some of the greatest minds in group-dynamics, latterly flowering into that seminal institution the National Training Laboratory of Arlington, Virginia. That movement revitalised the work of our own Tavistock Clinic and the groundbreaking insights of Bion (1961). Boyatzis' (1982) work on managerial competence was the continual subtext of the competency movement in the UK. The US Baldridge awards were regarded as a benchmark for British attempts to engender improvement in UK quality.

US authors still regard the UK as an important stomping ground to promote their ideas and their royalties. Tom Peters (Peters & Waterman, 1982), Gerard Egan (1994), Gary Hamel (1994), Warner Burke (1987) have all in the recent past made serious contributions on a wide canvas to the thinking of British business men and women. But not, apparently, to many of their actions.

The appearance of a new book with the word 'leadership' in its title would hardly be a novelty. The airport bookshops of the world are full of thoughtfully written and provocative books that encourage managers to emulate some eminent business leader or shift their perspectives to some distant future which is liberating, shocking or full of dancing giants. Our task is one of trying to help managers use ideas from previous thinkers and writers when the aeroplane has touched down, and when they find themselves engaging in 'real' activities, in complex organisations, with incessant demands for improvement, greater productivity or customer satisfaction.

The word 'complex' is not chosen without careful thought. The task of bringing about a demonstrable improvement in organisational effectiveness is never going to be easy. There are no universal panacea or simple approaches, save one. *Reject the ideas of anyone who claims that there are.* As someone once said, *To every complex problem there is a single simple solution – and it's always wrong!*

Our task in producing this book is neither to oversimplify nor to retreat into academic obscurantism. Rather, we are going to attempt to provide an analysis of the key factors to be considered in bringing about major change. Our intention is to move as quickly as possible to suggest guidelines for action, based upon our own work with organisations that have tried to effect significant change. It must be said, right from the outset, that such attempts have been more or less successful.

We make no claims for universal knowledge and truth. Perhaps an example will help put our position into clear focus. Since the mid-1980s we have both worked, one at the centre and one at the periphery, of an organisation that went through a profound and well-publicised set of developments – British Airways. We would not claim for one moment to have been the only or most important 'movers and shakers' but we were, in our own different ways, involved as people who were part of *making things better around here* rather than observers who can reflect and analyse from the sidelines. Calling the fall of the shot is an important activity, but deciding which shells to load and fire is a separate, more central and fundamental task.

To be more precise, the papers by Kotter and Leahey (1990) in

Harvard Case Studies, Goodstein and Burke (1991) in *Organizational Dynamics* and the book by Litwin et al (1996) represent valuable insights and reflections by experienced theorists who observe from afar. There is a place for such articles/books which contain much that is interesting but (and it is a very big but) articles like these represent a high level form of journalism. For us, the two articles are also full of inaccuracies which range from the trivial (incorrectly naming the organisation or its parts) to the more substantial, such as implying a segregated and linear thought process, which was never obvious to the key actors.

If we call such an approach 'journalistic' we mean it to be descriptive rather than pejorative. However, in whatever sense it is actually taken it means that less than full justice is being done to the complexity of the organisation involved or the tasks that had to be done to improve that organisation's effectiveness.

As we have said, between us we have over 60 years' accumulated life in and around organisations, variously as employees, management consultants, academic researchers, directors and even owners. This tally of life events has allowed us to see change, and the processes associated with bringing transformation about, in all its complexity. That experience encourages us to put pen to paper to elaborate and build upon our experience rather than exhort the reader to action – *You **must** do this* . . . or take an even more detached stance – *Studies have shown that* . . . Either approach would fail to do justice to the variety and complexity of issues involved and to belittle the efforts of the hundreds of committed men and women with whom we have worked on change processes of one kind or another and whose successes (oh, yes; and failures too) have informed and encouraged our thinking.

Hopefully our starting position is now clear. We will try, in the chapters that follow, to elaborate that which is complex about organisational performance improvement without oversimplifying. We hope to be able to show the reader who already knows that the issue is full of complexity, not that there are even more complications than he or she had never imagined, but how the ideas translate into a logical approach for action.

It is worth saying from the outset that this is not a book about British Airways. We see no reason why we should artificially restrict ourselves from using illustrations or anecdotes drawn from *The World's Favourite Airline* if they make a point, and we will do so from time to time. However, the central theme of the book is how to take the steps that move us forward towards organisations that become and remain more effective, rather than telling a particular story about a particular organisation at a particular point in time.

Although we will try to be clear as we go along there will almost certainly be times when the material reflects the whirling, buzzing, roller-coaster swooping confusion that we have personally experienced from working in real-time, really effective organisation improvement programmes. We considered a number of alternative titles in our attempts to be clear about what we were writing and whom we were writing it for. 'From soup to nuts' expressed the range of ideas but might have promised a cookery-book approach. 'Driving out organisational silliness' reflected our shared feeling that whatever else it might be, when it comes to organisational life 'common sense' appears to have nothing to do with the senses or to be particularly common!

We hope that we can act in the part of guides to walk with you through the landscape of our experience of organisational change. Not 'a guidebook' but more like 'a book by guides' for we are still learning and developing our ideas as we go. We have done our best to ensure that our ideas are informed by new research, codification, ideas, processes, procedures and insights, particularly those developed after 1985.

We are aware that the line between describing concepts and suggesting rationales for action may be a difficult one to tread. We feel passionately that the task is worth it. If organisations are to improve in increasingly global and competitive markets we need leaders and managers who can both think and do, with neither activity being seen as more important. The single quotation that best sums up our feeling on the matter is:

> The Society that scorns excellence in plumbing because it is a humble activity and tolerates shoddiness in philosophy because it is an exalted activity will have neither good plumbing nor good philosophy. Neither its pipes nor its theories will hold water.
>
> John W. Gardner (1984)

ON MODELS, MUDDLES AND MAPS

We have found it useful to organise our ideas around the linking structure provided by a model of organisation change. Like so many authors in this area we are indebted to the work of Morgan (1986). Morgan's work has helped us to understand that models of organisational functioning fall into many different classes.

Each class represents a *metaphor* for the way the creator of the model views the functioning of organisations. Thus, we find the metaphor of the organisation as a machine, an idea driven by the founding fathers of scientific management and profoundly influenced by the classical management theories of Fayol (1949) and Colonel Lyndall Urwick.

Morgan noted (pp 34–35) that the machine metaphor has both strengths and weaknesses. As he said *some organisations have had spectacular success using the mechanistic model.* In particular, organisations where there is a straightforward task to perform; where the environment is stable; where it is necessary to produce the same product time after time; when precision is at a premium and finally when the humans in the business are compliant. Morgan suggested that McDonald's hamburger chain has significantly benefited from the adoption of *scientific management* principles.

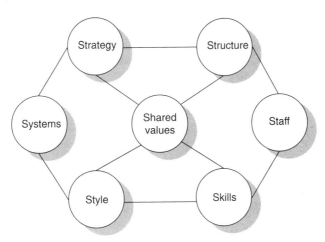

Figure 1.1 The Seven S model (from Pascale and Athos, 1981). Reprinted with permission.

However, the downside of these principles are often visible in the organisations with which we are familiar. Many were founded on mechanistic principles. Mechanistic organisational forms can have great difficulty in adapting to changing circumstances. Witness the traumas and outcry to recent changes in vision and purpose within the BBC. Too often we have all been subjected to the mindless and energy-sapping bureaucracy of many of our local authorities. When our needs as patients appear to be subordinated to the job descriptions and demarcations of the employees of our hospitals, we are experiencing a direct result of early Taylorism.

Finally, the disaffected, bored and dehumanised efforts of many British Rail employees attest again to a failure associated with designing an organisation as if it were a machine.

Chances are that the model of organisational functioning which is most familiar to our readers would be that known as the *Seven S*. Originally developed by Pascale and Athos (1981), it is best remembered for two reasons. First, the probably apocryphal story that it was developed on the back of an envelope, in a taxi, on the way to a meeting with clients.

Second, and most certainly not apocryphal, that it was used by Peters and Waterman in their seminal 1980s book *In Search of Excellence* as a framework within which to organise the data about their 20 or so 'excellent' organisations. In addition, Pascale and Athos (1981) used the model to urge US executives to use all seven elements omit in their groundbreaking exhortation entitled 'The Art of Japanese Management'. They saw a need for as much emphasis to be placed on the *Soft Ss* (Shared Values, Staff, Skills and Style) as on the remaining three *harder Ss*.

Definitions

- Strategy – Plans or courses of action leading to the allocation of an organisation's resources to reach identified goals.
- Structure – Characteristics of the organisation chart (functional, de-centralised, etc.).
- Systems – Procedures, routines and formalised ways of doing things.

- Staff – All the personnel within an organisation. Not just those in 'staff' as opposed to 'line' positions.
- Style – The typical and characteristic patterns of behaviour of managers which are reflected in the organisation's culture.
- Skills – The distinctive capabilities of employees.
- Shared Values – The meanings and 'guiding concerns' that an organisation imbues within its members.

The model has some immediate pragmatic benefits. It enables the enquiring analytical executive to 'dump' observations, reflections and even empirical data about the current state of an organisation into relatively discrete cells for the purpose of categorisation. Indeed, a recent author suggested erroneously that it was used by the executives of British Airways in their deliberations about that change programme. It was not (Hampden-Turner, 1990). However, Figure 1.2 illustrates how it might have been of value as a framework for categorising or 'dumping' perceptions.

Figure 1.2 illustrates two issues. First, the compelling simplicity of the *Seven Ss* framework for data disaggregation. Second, the framework's lack of utility in the formulation of a dynamic process of change from *what it is* to *what should be/might be*! Its limits are clear. Good plumbing? Perhaps. Weak philosophy? Undoubtedly. Good plumbers need to know where to begin!

IMPROVING THE PHILOSOPHY OF MODELLING

No model of organisational performance which has a true balance of pragmatism and intellectual rigour can afford to ignore open systems theory. Early ideas of management saw structures and relationships as permanent and enduring. As the decades have passed, however, managers have had to cope with increasing amounts of change, uncertainty and, perhaps above all else, greater and greater levels of complexity.

Some of this complexity will have come from within the organisation but much of it originated from without. The environment within which a business operates is increasingly influenced by

Seven S Item	British Airways in 1983	British Airways' aspirations
STRATEGY	• Highly dependent upon Government PSBR. • Fragmented attempts to improve 'the product'. • Simple market segmentation: First; business; second, visiting friends and relatives. • Keep in line with 'competitors' pricing'. • Don't upset the travel agents.	• Highly customer focused with elaborate market and customer research driving every product and service improvement. • Complex and highly researched brand differentiation with clear integration of psychological profiles of brand groups driving both physical product and customer-service delivery. • Employee empowering owner focused with eventually a global network and decentralisation of strategic business units.
SYSTEMS	• Recruitment and selection: Mass recruitment using tests, interviews and individual assessment. No sophisticated management assessment. • Training: Reasonable initial functional training, thereafter some more advanced, *but* by personal nomination and dominated by 'the blue-eyed boy syndrome'. • Performance appraisal: No systematic appraisal at any level. • Promotion: By seniority and 'dead men's shoes'. • Pay and collective bargaining: Over 150 different and overlapping pay scales. Negotiations dominated by employee-relations staff, who were seen as a 'law unto themselves'.	• Dedicated centralised recruitment selection for all staff. All management required to be assessed using independent psychological assessment. • In addition to functional training, large-scale corporate programmes for many levels of staff including MBAs and diplomas in business. • Compulsory performance appraisal system for top 2000 managers. • Promotion by assessment centre and individual profiling. Youngest 'high fliers' identified centrally. • Pay scales simplified; performance pay and profit share introduced; negotiations increasingly led by line managers.
STRUCTURE	• Highly functional and compartmentalised: engineering; pilots; cabin crew; catering; operations; finance; human resources.	• Realigned in the direction of customer service; seamless structure with marketing and operations providing the initial focus.
SHARED VALUES	• We're British, therefore best. • If the pilots ran this place it would be much better. • I wish they'd offer me voluntary severance. • Keep your head down and do as little as possible to avoid being noticed. • The Customer 'The Punter' is a pain.	• Putting people first. • Managers putting greater emphasis on people management. • The Customer pays our wages and deserves the best. • Customer-service front-line staff need to be respected because their work is not only onerous, but vital to our future success.

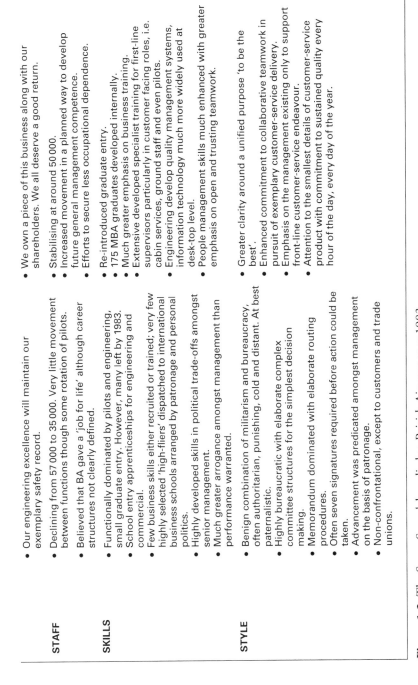

STAFF

- Our engineering excellence will maintain our exemplary safety record.
- Declining from 57 000 to 35 000. Very little movement between functions though some rotation of pilots.
- Believed that BA gave a 'job for life' although career structures not clearly defined.

- We own a piece of this business along with our shareholders. We all deserve a good return.
- Stabilising at around 50 000.
- Increased movement in a planned way to develop future general management competence.
- Efforts to secure less occupational dependence.

SKILLS

- Functionally dominated by pilots and engineering, small graduate entry. However, many left by 1983.
- School entry apprenticeships for engineering and commercial.
- Few business skills either recruited or trained; very few highly selected 'high-fliers' dispatched to international business schools arranged by patronage and personal politics.
- Highly developed skills in political trade-offs amongst senior management.
- Much greater arrogance amongst management than performance warranted.

- Re-introduced graduate entry.
- 175 MBA graduates developed internally.
- Much greater emphasis on business training.
- Extensive developed specialist training for first-line supervisors particularly in customer facing roles, i.e. cabin services, ground staff and even pilots.
- Engineering develop quality management systems, information technology much more widely used at desk-top level.
- People management skills much enhanced with greater emphasis on open and trusting teamwork.

STYLE

- Benign combination of militarism and bureaucracy, often authoritarian, punishing, cold and distant. At best paternalistic.
- Highly bureaucratic with elaborate complex committee structures for the simplest decision making.
- Memorandum dominated with elaborate routing procedures.
- Often seven signatures required before action could be taken.
- Advancement was predicated amongst management on the basis of patronage.
- Non-confrontational, except to customers and trade unions.

- Greater clarity around a unified purpose 'to be the best'.
- Enhanced commitment to collaborative teamwork in pursuit of exemplary customer-service delivery.
- Emphasis on the management existing only to support front-line customer-service endeavour.
- Attention to the smallest details of customer-service product with commitment to sustained quality every hour of the day, every day of the year.

Figure 1.2 The Seven S model applied to British Airways as at 1983.

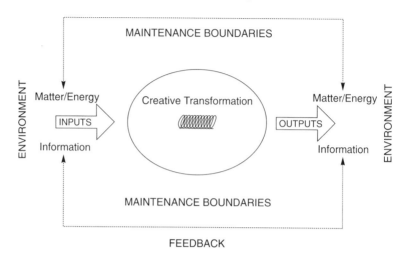

Figure 1.3 A generic open systems model.

legal, political and economic influences and an outward focus is essential for survival.

Open systems theory, originally founded in biological science, was the first theory that really addressed itself to the task of describing how an organisation adapted and developed within its environmental surroundings.

In its simplest form it sees work as a transformation process that requires inputs of material and resources and produces outcomes of goods or services, the whole being placed within a cyclical framework of feedback and the flow of material. Although the words seem intimidating, the idea is not complex and is well known to any small business owner – who will know that supplies of raw materials are needed for turning into finished product which must be supplied to the customer's satisfaction before the invoice can be raised to obtain the money that will allow the cycle to turn again.

We see more than a series of interlinked headings under which to categorise issues. The model shows both how the components are linked and how they work together as a total entity. Theoretically, a totally closed system could receive nothing from the environment and give nothing back. Such systems do not exist in nature or in

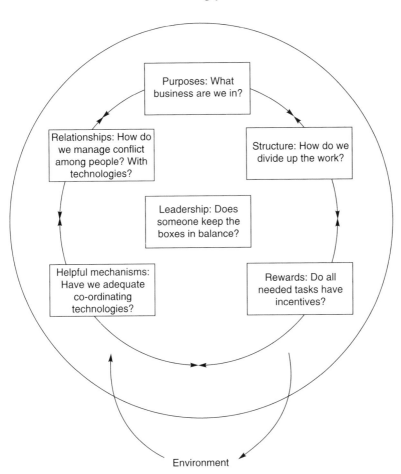

Figure 1.4 The Weisbord model (Weisbord, 1976). Reprinted by permission of the copyright holders, Sage Publications, Inc.

the world of commerce. The notion of feedback is particularly important. A thermostat working a central heating radiator will act once a pre-set temperature has been reached to cut off the flow of hot water and allow it to continue when the temperature then falls below a pre-determined level. Similarly, feedback in organisational terms is vital if a steady state is to be produced which gives an element of current stability, but an awareness of the need to change as a reaction to factors outside the boundary of the organisation itself.

An open systems model is more of a perspective than a theory, and particularly important as it shows how all aspects of work must fit within the totality of the organisation's adaptation to its environment.

Weisbord (1976) usefully developed the way of looking at organisational systems by subdividing what we have so far only considered as a central process of 'creative transformation'. He saw his model as performing a service something akin to that of a radar screen where the 'blips' can be seen which focus our direction onto good or bad highlights of behaviour. Be that as it may, for our purposes the important features of the model are:

- To emphasise the importance of the links with the external environment;
- To introduce some possible constructs (categories of ideas) that work to effect the transformation process; and
- The placing of leadership at a central position in the model. In Weisbord's view the principal task of leadership is to look for and correct any imbalance in the system.

The terms used by Weisbord are self-explanatory with perhaps the exception of his use of the term 'co-ordinating technologies' within the 'helpful mechanisms' component. He is not using the word 'helpful' in the sense of aiding, counselling or mentoring but as a form of cement that binds the organisation together. In these terms the co-ordinating technologies are the planning, budgetary and other systems that draw the efforts of many individuals together.

The model was designed to provide a form of route map for anyone coming across a new organisational situation that needed rapid understanding and diagnosis. It would not be fair to subject it to criticism for failing to provide deeper insights than it ever pretended to reveal. However, there are a couple of key points that need to be made to enable us to develop our argument as to what a more comprehensive model should contain.

First, leadership sits centrally but uncomfortably within the model. The word says 'leadership' but the implication of the role to be filled smacks more of co-ordinating manager. The title of this book makes it clear that we see leadership as being of prime importance and it is one that we will examine in Chapter Four in some detail.

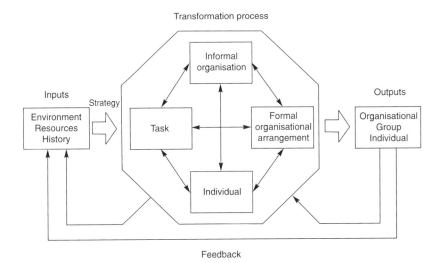

Figure 1.5 The Nadler and Tushman model (Nadler & Tushman, 1977. A diagnostic model for organization.) Reproduced with permission of the McGraw-Hill Companies. Copyright © 1977.

Second, the internal components of the model are seen as working in a circular fashion with single inputs and outputs. It is not clear how the external environment acts to effect the process, whether one component may influence more than simply the next one in the circle or where one should start to 'break-in' to get some radical change rather than simply preserving the measured and balanced form of status quo.

Weisbord's major interest was in using the model to examine how far the formal and informal aspects of an organisation's functioning were in kilter. To make more progress we need some form of model that specifies these issues with more precision, while saying more about the possible interactions of the individual components believed to be contributing to effective organisational performance. Such a model was provided by Nadler and Tushman (1977).

Nadler and Tushman followed the line we have been developing of seeing organisations as open systems and thus influenced by their environments. Their prime concern, hence the idea of congruence, was to produce a model that allowed components to be examined in terms of how they fitted with each other. Thus areas of incongruence would be obvious springboards for direct initial action. For our current purposes, however, the major interest is in the way the Nadler and Tushman model further elaborated the central components which might be seen as leading to effective organisational performance.

Nadler and Tushman have produced a model which is clearly more complex. Their obvious interest in developing insights into the difference between the formal and informal aspects of organisational life is reflected by their choice of variables to position at the very centre of their model. The developments that we see as being more important in adding to a general model of organisational effectiveness are:

- The specification of input and output variables which were only referred to in passing by Weisbord.
- The introduction of strategy (deliberately and formally derived or produced informally and without great initial thought) as an important variable.
- The positioning of the feedback loop.
- The identification of three different levels of analysis – organisational, group and individual.

The ways in which the dynamics between the central parts of the systems might operate are not examined in detail, and the role of leadership is left unexplained other than presumably having had a hand in the production of a strategy and in the operation of organisational arrangements.

Both Weisbord and Nadler and Tushman have concentrated on the distinction between informal and formal aspects of organisational functioning. Without wishing to be too critical this may have taken their eyes away from a more precise and formal definition of the factors that in a more general sense both 'influence' and lead to organisational outcomes. These are areas that can be addressed with the help of a third model that further builds on and develops the two we have examined so far.

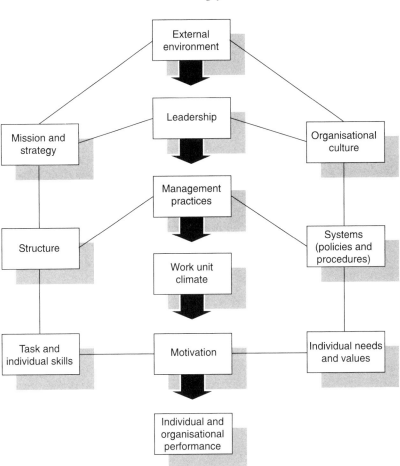

Figure 1.6 The Burke–Litwin model (Burke & Litwin, 1989). Reproduced by permission of Warner Burke Associates Inc.

THE BURKE–LITWIN MODEL

The Burke–Litwin (1989) model aims to move the representation of what goes on in an organisation away from the level of description and more towards one that can be used to predict behaviour and the consequences of behaviour on performance. The authors were W. Warner Burke of Teachers College, Columbia University, New York, and George Litwin, then a professor of Harvard Business School.

The model has four major features which are different from the other open systems models we have looked at in this chapter:

- It attempts to describe associations between significant organisational levers in the sense of causation rather than just association.
- Its components are arranged hierarchically. That is, issues that are of most potency in influencing the success or otherwise of organisational outcomes are to be found at the top of the model.
- It is more than a graphical representation. Burke and Litwin have produced an impressive body of research evidence to support the linkages employed in the model (Burke & Litwin, 1992).
- The model clearly differentiates between transformational and transactional factors. Burke and Litwin see mission and strategy, leadership and culture as factors which are transformational. By transformational they imply that these factors are the ones which are initially impacted by environmental change and that it is through these variables that major organisation change must be wrought. The factors lower in the model, labelled transactional, are those which are necessary but not sufficient to bring about radical or transformational change.

We happily acknowledge the considerable debt we owe to the Burke–Litwin model for shaping our thinking and ways of organising the material we have tried to present to others to help them fashion significant change in their organisations. We have gathered some perspectives that encourage us to add a fourth in the line of open system models.

In doing so, we are trying to reflect the following emphases:

- That leadership is the key dimension rather than being one of three important but equal transformational variables. Archimedes reportedly claimed '*Give me but one firm spot on which to stand, and I will move the earth*'. For us, the fulcrum of organisational change is the point at which the external environment most pointedly meets the organisational boundary, and the lever is leadership.
- We see what Burke and Litwin call *Management Practices* more like *Leadership in Action*. The words themselves are not a major concern, it is the point about the specification of behaviour that

matters. In our view, management practices are the mechanisms through which the leadership of an organisation shapes the behaviours which are appropriate for developing the culture and which drives the day-to-day actions and procedures that will ultimately affect both individual, group and organisation performance. Thus, we position management practices as one of the transformational variables rather than a transactional variable.

- In perhaps a not dissimilar fashion, the distinction between organisational culture on the one hand and aspects of mission and strategy on the other are too artificially distanced from the leadership process. We would want to emphasise the idea that the transformational processes are individually definable, and certainly have strong individual implication for how subsequent structures and systems are devised, but that they are closely linked conceptually and are an integral part of the leadership process.
- The distinction between organisational, group and individual levels of analysis so clearly made by Nadler and Tushman needs bringing more clearly into focus.

THE GEORGIADES AND MACDONELL MODEL

Incorporating these changes brings us to the model that will be used to shape and inform the presentation of our ideas in the remainder of this book. Out of a sense of continuity with its antecedents rather than any lack of modesty it seems sensible to call it the Georgiades and Macdonell Model of Organisational Effectiveness.

Our prime contentions should come as no great surprise to the reader by now. We hold that for an organisation to overlook, even for a minute, the potency of the influences at work from the immediate external environment, is to be at risk from forces and circumstances that could be catastrophic to the organisation.

The model clearly extends and elaborates the earlier Burke–Litwin attempt. We make clear that we see the role of leadership as central with four explicit imperatives.

- The scrutiny of the external environmental factors.
- The development of a vision and the articulation of the strategic implications of that vision.

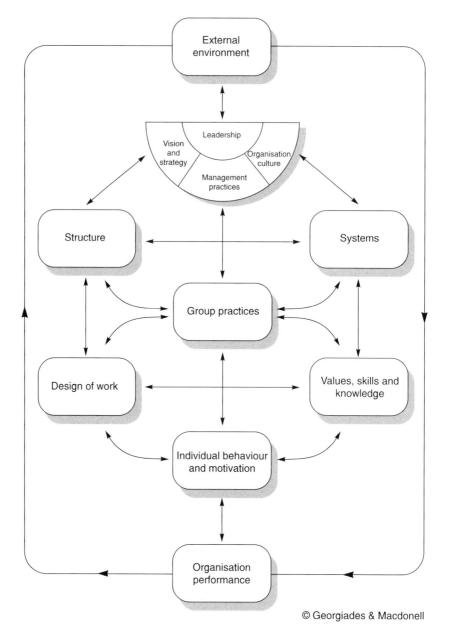

Figure 1.7 The Georgiades and Macdonell model of organisation effectiveness.

- The development of the appropriate culture to meet the needs of the vision and strategy.
- The specification of the required management practices which drive the desired culture.

In addition we make more explicit the role of work design in the lower position of the model, in essence to balance the recruitment, selection and training implications around the notion of motivation. Finally, we relabel the original group climate variable to encompass the notion of group practices. While Burke and Litwin (1989) make the distinction between 'climate' and 'culture' quite explicit, practitioners coming to the distinction for the first time often find it unhelpful. To continue the notion of practices (the way group members behave) is in our experience more helpful.

The model satisfies the need for sound philosophy. Burke and Litwin's extensive literature review cannot be faulted, save perhaps by pedants. Given the inherent limitations of complex organisational research they have delivered as tight a representation of the empirical reality as one could wish for. We shall add our own empirical data to the argument later in the book.

However, our major concern here is its value as a tool for plumbing. How helpful is it? Does it aid in the understanding of organisational complexity? Does it make the planning of a transformation easier? What are the pragmatic limits of its use?

The best way of approaching answers to these questions will be by illustration. We will take two well-known events, one general and one specific to organisational change, and show how the important factors and influences can be grouped and examined under the headings of the Georgiades and Macdonell model.

THE *CHALLENGER* ACCIDENT OF 1986

Some analysts of the events preceding and the circumstances surrounding the fatal explosion of space shuttle *Challenger* in January 1986 have differed from the conclusions of the Presidential Commission established by President Reagan. That Commission said that the accident was caused by a failure in the joint between the two lower segments of the right solid rocket motor. They also said that a contributing cause of that accident was that 'the decision to launch the Challenger was flawed' *Presidential Commission Report, July 1986 Vol. 1 pp 40 and 82.*

It is instructive to use the G and M model to analyse both that document in detail and other evidence. Such an analysis indicates, among other things, that there were significant *external environment* pressures acting upon the NASA leadership immediately prior to the launch decision. Among these were:

- Significant cost cutting demands from both government and taxpayers.
- The need to ensure that the space shuttle programme was both competitive, lucrative and timely.
- Constant carping, media criticism and cynicism about NASA's competence.
- The need to maximise the public relations impact of the launch, which was to include the first US private citizen in space, Ms Christa McAuliffe the teacher.
- The need for President Reagan 'the great communicator' to be able to address the American people on television either before or during the State of the Union Address for that year and to be able to talk live to the astronauts.

And finally the most literal external environmental demand:

- the quite exceptional low temperature weather reports from the Cape, as well as bad sea conditions, which forced the withdrawal of rescue ships from probable splash-down locations in the Atlantic.

Additional external environment demands were facing Morton Thiokol, a supplier to NASA (a significant party to the decision to launch). These were that:

- Morton Thiokol were facing the need to retender for their contract on the shuttle boosters.
- Their customer, NASA, was demanding higher levels of contract compliance and customer satisfaction.

It is in this context that NASA made the fateful decision to fly. However, further examination using the model as a template indicates that NASA leadership had failed to grasp the significance of the transformational process that was required as a result of the space shuttle endeavour. For instance, the vision of the organisation had necessarily moved from one driven mostly by research, development and exploration to one where the primary goal was 'commercialised' freighter operation.

The impact of this change meant that at an operational level the organisation committed itself initially to fly 60 flights per year and then more realistically to 24 flights per year. The schedule for the flights has now being determined by the needs of customers external to NASA. Previously, NASA determined flight schedules on the basis of its own internal research, development and operational needs. Now, it had to satisfy the customer in order to meet explicit commercial demands. Productivity and safety standards had in the past been driven by internal directives. Now they were determined by commercial reality. There is no evidence that the leadership undertook systematically to communicate these changes in vision, nor to build a strategy which would take account of their new world. On the contrary, there is evidence to suggest that the very opposite is the case. The numbers of staff in safety, for the inspection of suppliers, for general reliability and for quality assurance were actually reduced.

An analysis of the prevailing organisation culture at NASA compounds the problem. As a result no doubt of 20-plus years of extraordinary success, of '25 years doing the impossible' which included putting the first man on the moon; rescuing the apparently doomed Apollo 13; having an extraordinarily low astronaut mortality rate, with many hundreds of successful launches and vanquishing the Russian competition, the prevailing culture of NASA was of an agency which believed in its own invincibility.

Culturally NASA's members were proud and invulnerable. They believed themselves to be infallible. They were the 'can-do agency'. Additionally, like most Federal agencies, they were highly bureaucratic and heavily layered. At Marshall, located in Alabama, where the fatal decision concerning the O-ring (identified as the engineering cause of the *Challenger* accident) was ultimately made, the culture was compounded by a long history of autocratic and fear-dominated injunctions. Perhaps the worst of these was issued by the head of Marshall at his inaugural speech in which he said that 'Marshall would never be the reason for delaying a launch' while he was boss. Marshall had as its founding father, Hitler's right-hand rocket man, Werner von Braun.

These cultural phenomena all played a significant part in the fatal decision to launch that January day in 1986. No evidence exists, that we know of, that the leadership at NASA actively pursued, as part of their leadership responsibilities, a review of the prevailing culture and the extent to which that culture was aligned to the new, more challenging, externally driven mission.

One example of failing to drive an articulation of management practices will suffice. Despite the fact that senior members of NASA knew that rescue ships had been withdrawn from the Atlantic; that the ambient temperatures at the Cape had, the night before launch, provoked the use of de-icing crews and that there was concern about lack of research on low temperature effects on the critical O-ring; it was *not* the practice to inform the crew of the flight of these factors. It was not the management practice to include the flight captain or any member of the crew in the decision to launch. They were not part of the loop.

The seven astronauts who died that day were totally unaware of any of the issues which contributed to their deaths; issues which were known, considered and ultimately ignored by the NASA leadership. A comparable situation in civil aviation, in which the flight crew were not a party to the decision to take-off is inconceivable. And yet at NASA, prior to 1986, such a management practice was the norm.

In conclusion, a post-facto analysis of what led up to the events of the fateful January day is greatly facilitated by using an integrating model along the lines of the one we offer. At the very least the model offers a set of pegs on which the range of 'being wise after the event' issues can be hung. More usefully, the model offers insights into the way that seemingly unconnected happenings can be seen as coming together. Most importantly to us, the analysis reveals a picture that managers as well as consultants and OD practitioners can transfer to other settings and hopefully see ways of informing future decisions to avoid the mistakes of the past.

PUTTING PEOPLE FIRST AT BRITISH AIRWAYS

A second illustration of the utility of the model, this time in the design of large-scale organisation interventions can be drawn from the early work at British Airways. The case of the BA turnaround, as we have noted elsewhere, is frequently cited in textbooks and in colour supplements. The most frequently cited aspect of that early process was called 'Putting People First' (PPF).

PPF is often described as a customer-service training course for all staff. The programme did, of course, include references to customer-service issues. One chapter of the book of the course was devoted to a *Three Minute Customer Service Course*. On the basis of these elements external observers assumed that that was both the content and the intent of PPF. In short, that it was designed primarily to meet needs identified in the values, skills and knowledge box of the G and M model. It did, in fact, do much more. The programme, which ultimately was delivered to 40 000 employees over a two-year period, dealt directly with all four variables highlighted in the leadership box of the G and M model.

First, PPF challenged some deep-seated cultural issues. The prevailing culture of BA in 1984 was derived from its military and civil service origins. Many job titles included reference to military rank, for instance, officer or superintendent; most people worked in branches and not departments and went on leave not on holiday or vacation. The dominant management culture included the use of the initials of the job (CX for Chief Executive; DP for Director of Personnel) and rules about writing memos which required multiple sign-off for transmission upward. The rules for PPF began a wholesale onslaught upon these cherished 'ways of doing things around here'.

First, participants were requested not to attend in uniform. Immediately therefore symbols of rank were not evident. Secondly, participants were randomly allocated to sub-groups. Parties of work-mates arriving together were spread about the large auditorium. Any one sub-group might have contained a customer-service person from Terminal One, two members of cabin crew, one long-haul, one short-haul, a Concorde pilot and a middle manager from marketing and so on.

During the course of PPF each sub-group was challenged to solve problems relating to some aspect of airline performance. They did so naturally, without deference to rank, position or power. PPF began a process that suggested that all of the folks were 'in this together' and no one individual department, function or rank was precluded from making a contribution to making things better. The process was not highlighted. The experience, however, was persuasive. Few could escape the reality of these small groups. But nobody actually said 'I have seen the enemy and it is us!' Getting things done seemed more highly valued for those few hours than whose signature was on the memo or whose backside had to be covered.

Such unfreezing, gentle and unthreatening as it was, laid the foundations of more significant culture change activities that were to follow.

But PPF did more. It planted firmly the notion that the survival of BA was dependent on caring. Caring for yourself; caring for your colleagues and ultimately caring for the customers, who in the cultural patois of the time, were known as 'punters'.

What followed thereafter, presented on multiple occasions by the Chief Executive (no less) was a restatement of 'what could be'. Sir Colin Marshall held his audience spellbound. Night after night, week after week (he in fact closed about 95% of all PPF programmes) the Chief Executive laid out a new vision. No Martin Luther King he! This was no tub-thumping oratory. But it was honourable rhetoric. Slowly, simply and with complete faith Sir Colin Marshall essentially described a future in which all those present could make a contribution. Caring for each other, caring for the customer, meant ultimately success for all. His behaviour, particularly in his willingness to listen attentively, often making notes in his small pocket notepad, and to respond directly and without humbug to direct questions, was in itself culturally challenging.

The director who had on occasions to step in, as substitute for the Chief Executive, felt the visible sigh of disappointment from the audience, as the substitution was announced late on the second day of the programme. This was no easy understudying role. The notion of a critical mass had become a reality. The research follow-up confirms this idea. While the programme had been entertaining, many, particularly the customer service folk, the group to attend first, thought it a bit like 'teaching grandmother to suck eggs'. In the end, however, they recognised that corporate success would come if they focused single-mindedly on satisfying the customers.

Sir Colin implied and gave hope. Not through the usual panoply of corporate communications, no cascade briefing, no rehearsed and scripted videotape. In many ways, he assessed the need perfectly. What the situation required was real visible and human interaction. The establishment of a bridgehead of trust, viable only by eyeball-to-eyeball interaction. Those of us, who understudied the role, for the odd occasions when Sir Colin Marshall could not do it himself, will recall also the heavyweight interrogation which followed every Wednesday or Friday morning as Sir Colin sought to understand what the folks had had on their minds.

For many BA employees this was no phoney attempt to 'con' them into something dreamt up by the bosses. It was a true watershed. A break from the past so significant that 30 000-plus employees participated in the revitalisation of their airline. Nor was it for Marshall an exercise designed to promote his persona. It was not an activity dedicated to his power, but to the power of all of those present who wanted to be part of something special. And many did!

The work that followed from PPF involved many hundreds of airline staff who collectively contributed over 700 improvements to customer service, through Customer First Teams, during the following three years. Many observers, both entrepreneurs and scholars, have over the intervening years wildly misinterpreted the true 'purpose' of Putting People First. Others have tried to replicate its content. Most have failed to bring about the transformation that it accomplished with BA. Some because they believed that no Chief Executive should devote such a large block of time to this kind of internal 'public relations activity'. Others, because to attend a training course week after week 'could not be justified'. Others because they could not articulate such a human and uncomplicated vision. Still more, perhaps, because they felt that they had little to learn from such an exercise.

Our post-facto analysis confirms the belief that we had at the time, that PPF was no training course in customer-service skills, but an intervention operating at the transformational level. It challenged old cultural norms, and replaced them with a new and more egalitarian discourse; it provided a new vision of what could be, delivered by leadership that cared and was prepared to listen and then to act. For all employees, in real-time and face to face. Some skills training course!

SUPPORTING EVIDENCE

Recently we received some interesting and confirmatory evidence to support in broad terms the power of this model. Kotter (1995) published an insightful and empirical investigation into the reasons for the failure of large-scale organisation transformation. He noted that over the last decade he had observed more than 100 companies who have 'tried to remake themselves'. Amongst these he cites Ford, Bristol Myers Squibb, General Motors, British Airways and Eastern Airlines. In each case he asserts that their basic goal has been to make changes in the way business was conducted in order to cope with 'a new, more challenging market environment'. Our model suggests that not merely 'market' environments represent pressure for change but all aspects of the external environment might seem more accurate. In the BA case for example, while the market was demanding change, so was the Government and so were financial institutions in the run up to privatisation. So too were the British public, whether or not they were customers.

Kotter outlined eight major sources of potential failure. Each can be seen to fit neatly and hierarchically into the G and M model.

The first four in his order were a failure to:

1. Establish a sense of urgency.
2. Form a powerful guiding coalition.
3. Create a vision (and the strategies to create the vision).
4. Communicate vision (and the strategies).

All four of these injunctions are represented in the G and M model as part of the transformational levers but for us the second of Kotter's issues is pre-eminent. No single CEO can express the needs (demands) of the external environment in compelling and urgent terms as well as express and communicate a vision and strategy alone without assistance. What Kotter calls a 'guiding coalition' we suggest is better described as a 'driving alliance'. This is no mere matter of semantics. The potency of what this group will need to achieve must be reflected in the power of the words used to describe them. Kotter's description could appear to mean a group of benign influential organisational godparents, waiting in the wings until needed. The word coalition does not convey for us the shared idea of 'hanging together or hanging alone' that is implicit with the use of the word 'alliance' and which must be clear to whoever accepts membership of the leading group. In a similar vein the word 'guiding' is too detached, uninvolved or neutral for what the members of that group will have to do. Guides can be useful but need not be central and fully committed members of the party – drivers must be.

Kotter's fifth injunction suggested 'empowering others to act on the vision'. Here he cited the needs to remove obstacles to change. Probably the single most potent obstacle to transformation is the prevailing culture of the enterprise. But so too are lack of alignment between systems and structure and the vision. Empowering others is accomplished by proscribing management practices and aligning systems (procedures) and structures.

Kotter's sixth, seventh and eighth points were:

6. Planning for and creating short-term wins.
7. Consolidating improvement and creating still more change.
8. Institutionalising new approaches.

He wrote of the needs to 'recognise and reward' employees; to change systems, structures and policies that don't fit the vision as well as 'hiring, promoting and developing employees who can implement the vision'.

In short he proceeded stepwise to the lowest levels of the G and M model. Iteration through the model is implicit as cycles of change, consolidation and institutionalisation are advised as the way forward.

Explicitly he failed only to recognise the power of team practices as a significant part of the transformation process. However, Kotter's contribution reconfirms our faith in the power of our model to help line managers come to terms not only with the substance of transformational change but also its critical order. It would be inconceivable to either Kotter or ourselves that you might build and communicate a vision prior to the establishment of a significant driving alliance.

We have recently become aware of a school of academic thinking and writing that challenges many of the assumptions that are implicit in this chapter. The suggestion by authors such as Thierry Pauchant (1996) is that management and organisations are in crisis. So far, we are in agreement. However, the nature of the crisis, these writers suggest, is in the failure of organisations first to provide meaning for people at work and secondly in the myth of what they call 'organisational perfection'. One proposition, for instance, suggests that the economic criteria of organisation success will necessarily make a mockery of multicultural, ethical and ecological concerns. Further, that the establishment of 'self-defeating' success goals such as excellence or zero-defects, or even simply being 'best-in-class' are self-destructive. Worse yet, that being outstanding means inevitably the crucifixion of leaders and disillusionment of followers. That organisations whose leadership sets out to establish visions of competitive excellence will become disillusioned and burnt out. That to deny the possibility of human fallibility is illusory. Such an illusion, strongly promulgated and reified, leads in time to the defeat of the human spirit and the emergence of a Jungian shadowside of organisational life. In short, visionary leadership is a massive con-trick, conceived to dupe the unwary, simple-minded employee whose role in life is merely to follow the ringmaster.

By observation, we know of organisations where such phenomena occur. We could not deny that reality for many employees. However, our propositions in this book attempt to recognise and promote some alternative theories in action. In short, it does not always have to be that way.

Our next chapter will devote itself to issues connected with the external environment. Rather than keep the debate at the same level of general explanation that has, of necessity, been employed in this first chapter, we will endeavour to make good our promise to develop some guidelines for actions.

Chapters One and Two together serve as a necessary introduction to our model, philosophy and approach. Chapter Three deals with the issue of measuring and capturing the views of a major, though often overlooked, stakeholder – the employee. Chapter Four examines the long and sometimes tortuous history of ideas about leadership, but with a view to opening up what has sometimes been a rather sterile and semantic debate about the difference between 'leadership' and 'management'. This will be the longest chapter in the book and we make no apology for this in view of the central place the topic must occupy.

We will show how an understanding of leadership demands close consideration of vision and strategy (Chapter Five), the exigencies of building an adaptive organisational culture (Chapter Six) and on, most importantly, to the development of management practices that turn values into behaviours that are appropriate in the sense of being aligned with all the organisational ambitions (Chapter Seven). We said at the start of this chapter that we would try to produce some guidelines for action. These will constitute our final chapter (Chapter Eight).

Chapter Two
SCANNING THE EXTERNAL ENVIRONMENT

AN INTRODUCTION

Our introductory chapter outlined the thinking and development of ideas that lay behind the model we are going to employ to structure all that follows. Logically our starting point cannot be anything other than to examine the external environment within which an organisation operates. This, of course, gives rise to a particular problem of presentation and, indeed, thinking. When we see information in clusters and boxes we naturally look within them and at the arrows that join one with another. It is a lot more difficult to look into the 'space between'.

The difficulty is reflected in the way that many employees prefer not to look too far outside the bounds of their own function or department for fear of the anxiety-provoking uncertainty they will find. The very jargon of current business approaches offers little in the way of comfort and certainty: down-sizing, right-sizing, re-engineering, merger and acquisition do not convince people that they live in a stable and predictable environment where change will be slow, natural, pleasant and, perhaps above all, predictable. Of course, some employees find all this to be the very meat and drink of their careers and development. However, to possibly less educated, able or flexible people, the threats to the total substance of their lives is profound and significant.

It has been, in the not too distant past, possible to think of organisational environments as ranged along a continuum of turbulence and complexity. The influential writers Emery and Trist suggested as long ago as 1965 that such a continuum could be represented by definitions such as:

- Placid-randomised environments – In which demands are randomly distributed and change occurs slowly. It is hard to think of many environments which even come close to this definition these days. A small country-town solicitors' practice or the Lloyd's market before 1990 might have come close.
- Placid-clustered environments – Where again change occurs slowly but where threats may come from customers or competitors forming a cohesive threat. In current circumstances, recently privatised utilities offer an example of this position on the continuum.
- Disturbed-reactive environments – Where there may be many competitors all seeking the same market potentially dominated by one or two 'large players'. The need here is for flexibility and to be able to evolve new tactics as new circumstances come into view. In the UK this is the type of environment in which travel agents find themselves operating.
- Turbulent-field environments – Where the only steady state is change. Organisations continually have to adapt to changes in customers, suppliers and products. Perhaps the world of business systems and software is the obvious example here.

The key message contained in looking at how Emery and Trist's thinking has stood the test of the passage of well over 30 years is the obvious one of how many organisations find themselves increasingly moving towards more turbulence. This is not really the place to examine in great detail why this might be; the whole thrust of a commercial world where economies are now seen in global terms, where technological changes come at an ever more rapid rate, where pollution and environmental awareness in the sense of being 'green' are of increasing concern and where loyalty is not a concept employers can expect, let alone demand, must all add to the push away from placid states to turbulent fields.

The problem for many managements, and individual managers, has been one of trying to comprehend all these external changes, let alone their implications of what might need to be done within the organisation. It is clear that crossing your fingers and hoping that there is no one out there with a team of accountants reviewing your financial returns and sizing you up as a takeover target is a strategy that was not even much use to the ostrich. Thus, the task must be how to impose some order onto chaos. We have found it useful to start with an examination of the stakeholders, that is the group of organisations or individuals who have an interest (which could be formal or informal, legitimate or otherwise) in the continuing existence and success of an organisation. To make the point about what we mean by stakeholders, consider the possible range of people and organisations who could be so considered in Figure 2.1.

The listing in Figure 2.1 illustrates the complexity. The potential turbulence created might seem endless. The list is awesome; however, it is merely illustrative. To make matters worse, the rate of change for each of the stakeholders or of the wider influences may also be exponential. Turbulent field indeed! Must effective leadership monitor and respond to all influences simultaneously? Can some be assigned to the pending tray for their monthly review? Does the functional expertise within an organisation take explicit and formal responsibility for scanning in its area of responsibility? And if that is the case who scans the scanners? *Quis custodiet ipsos custodes?*

Often events far beyond the boundary of the business may bring it to its knees. Such was the case in 1986 when President Reagan used the USAF located in the United Kingdom to bomb the Libyan capital. The impact of that one decision had convulsive effects upon the management of British Airways. In all respects and overnight the airline was faced with a critical and significant loss of its US market. Early calculations indicated a potential loss of millions of pounds of budgeted revenue, amounting to approximately £50 million of bottom-line profit.

Citizens of the United States decided that Europe was unsafe. They cancelled their personal travel plans. US corporations cancelled business travel, unless absolutely necessary, and then only with corporate presidential permission and on US carriers. No amount of formal stakeholder scanning could have forewarned BA's directors of the impending turbulence in their affairs. There were no crystal balls which could have foreseen these events. No strategy department, even full to overflowing with prestigious MBAs, would have been able to foresee such consequences. The extent to which organisations cope or do not cope with such events, is not then a function of the extent of their capacity for forward prediction, but on other aspects of the organisation's (or driving leadership alliance's) strengths and weaknesses. In the BA case, an inventive marketing campaign in the USA, together with an adaptive culture within the company, produced outcomes inconceivable to the key actors at the start of the affair.

HOW THEN CAN WE REDUCE THE OVERLOAD?

Our experience, together with a myriad of senior managers exposed to these ideas, led us to conclude that at the very least it may be possible to identify those stakeholders who must hold our fairly constant, immediate and regular attention.

Why not try this exercise with your colleagues? List (in any order and without discussion) all the potential stakeholders of your business. Then ask each person to rank the top five in importance to the success of the business. Compare notes! Our best guess will be that within the top five, three stakeholders will always get a significant number of votes.

These are:

- Shareholders (owners, pension funds, the City, etc.).
- Customers (and the customers of customers).
- Staff.

Depending upon the type of organisation we may also need to include suppliers and industry regulatory bodies.

The important point to grasp here is not just that there are three key stakeholder groups, but that their relationship is essentially dynamic and marked by necessary tension and conflict of interest. The word 'conflict' is not meant to imply interpersonal dislike but the idea that one group can only meet all of its own requirements at the expense of one or both of the others.

If a supermarket decides to improve its customer service by opening more check-out desks, either staff have to work longer hours for the same pay, or extra money has to be raised that would

Grouping	PLC company e.g. an airline	Public agency e.g. hospital
Customers or consumers or clients	Customers Shareholders	The public Patients and their families General practitioners Research community
Suppliers	Banks and insurance companies Trade unions Providers of goods/services Advertising, marketing Agencies Auditors Business consultants Finance community (including Stock Exchange)	Labour market (including doctors and nurses) Sub-contracted services Drug companies Donors Taxpayers
Other organisations	Competitors Regulators Legislators Courts Health and safety inspectors International law makers CAA Community groups (environmental)	The Department of Health Community Health Councils Medical profession Volunteer groups Trust Boards Community groups Legislators Police Social Work agencies

Other groups whose influence may be less direct	Research and development community The universities The Patents Office Public lobby or pressure groups Consumer organisations The media	Drug licensing authorities The universities and research communities Advanced technology research – especially pharmacology Research grant trusts Special needs groups (cancer etc.) The media
Wider social/ economic influences	International trade Oil price fluctuation Domestic business climate Market trends Interest rates Industry structure, international and domestic Securities market Trade practices Auditing standards Population demography Legislation (including subsidies) Taxation provision Environmentalism Impact of foreign policy of foreign governments	Public attitudes (especially to sickness prevention) General government provision for special groups (the elderly and children) Population demography Public sanitation and housing policy Court decisions General trends in health care costs Tax revenues associated with domestic business climate Alternative health care providers (private medicine and fringe medicine)

Figure 2.1 A matrix of stakeholders.

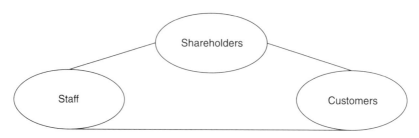

Figure 2.2 The stakeholder trinity.

otherwise have been due to the shareholders. If the shareholders demand profit maximisation, the extra money (assuming a moderately 'steady state') can only come from paying less to the staff or raising more from the customers.

This 'trinity' of interested parties may be illustrated in the simple diagram shown as Figure 2.2. The diagram provides the focus to comprehend not only where demands from the external environment may be coming, but also makes it crystal clear that an organisational response which is simply swinging to meet a specific demand or influence is almost certain to be too simplistic, and a source of further turbulence, when all the stakeholder groups start to feel affected.

All well and good, but these ideas are necessarily pitched at the highest, most general and abstract of organisational analysis. One of the keys to developing organisational effectiveness is the way in which every member of the organisation, and we do mean *every member*, is aware of what behaviour is required of him or her to meet the current objectives. It is still not uncommon to hear potentially committed employees talk sadly of the way they have to cross the road to buy a copy of the local newspaper for information about orders won, profits made or redundancies predicted.

Many organisations have tried communicating company results in a variety of ways with a variety of success. In our experience they have often given up or felt the need to moderate what they say because they feel they cannot trust subordinates to keep business information confidential or that they simply will not be able to understand the ideas behind financial ratios and balance sheet data.

The first of these objections will be dealt with a little later on. It is worth simply planting the thought, before moving on, that if you trust an employee with several thousand pounds' worth of equipment or to talk to significant customers, why would you have any reason to suppose that they would senselessly 'sell you out'?

If there is a problem of understanding then that is surely a problem for the communicator of the information rather than blaming the recipient? People who believe that their workforce neither cares nor understands what organisational success looks like should try the experiment of following some of their employees around on a Saturday afternoon. The chances are that many of them will be found in cold, wet, uncomfortable sporting venues, shouting themselves hoarse in support of whatever team in whatever sport takes their fancy. You can be absolutely certain that they know what the difference between success and failure looks like. With even a rudimentary knowledge of the rules of the game, most will also be able to tell you with great clarity what winning means and how to recognise success when it comes. We talk happily about 'goals' in business terms. For most employees the term is not a strange or novel one. What they miss in their work settings is the information to let them know whether or not the business is 'winning'.

THE BALANCED SCORECARD

This idea has been developed and extended by Kaplan and Norton (1992 and 1993) in two papers that describe what they call the *Balanced Scorecard*. They also take the view that external turbulence is such that no single measure can help focus attention on the key indices of success, and also that there is no 'one best' measure capable of providing a clear performance target or focus on critical areas of the business. Managers, they believe, want a balanced presentation of more than one set of measures. Their research with a number of companies 'at the leading edge' of performance has led them to devise a set of four measures (the balanced scorecard) that can give top management a fast but comprehensive view of the business.

The balanced scorecard they derived allows managers to look at their business from four important perspectives:

- How do customers see us? (customer perspective).
- What must we excel at? (internal perspective).
- Can we continue to improve and create value? (innovation and learning perspective).
- How do we look to shareholders? (financial perspective).

This classification seems to mirror the 'trinity' of major stakeholders we elaborated earlier. The customer and shareholder perspectives are clear enough, the place for the staff is less immediately apparent, but becomes clear enough within the remaining half of the 'scorecard' when individual items are examined. We reproduce a copy of an example scorecard produced by Kaplan and Norton from their work within Rockwater to make the point (Figure 2.3).

Kaplan and Norton's idea helps to cut through much of the complexity faced by anyone trying to juggle with the uncertainties coming from the external environment and from within their own organisation. What it does not do is help us to reduce the issues to the level of understanding needed by everyone in the organisation if they are to be able to *align their behaviour in the direction of meeting organisational goals* or, in the simpler language we prefer, *know if they are winning*.

A way forward that seemed particularly useful in our estimation (and which considerably predated Kaplan and Norton) was to develop the potential of collecting feedback from survey data which could be used to provide clear and understandable 'are we winning?' data to go alongside the more apparently 'hard' (yet easy to understand) financial data. Interestingly, our experience in working with managers of considerable seniority has been that they seldom really understood the terms in which financial data were presented to them (just what does 'return on capital employed' mean?) and were simply too anxious about showing the 'weakness' to go out and demand explanation or alternative data that they could understand. If the senior management do not really know what 'winning' looks like then it is hardly surprising that the ideas are not passed down the line.

The idea of getting feedback from customers and employees by the use of questionnaire techniques is scarcely new but the tendency

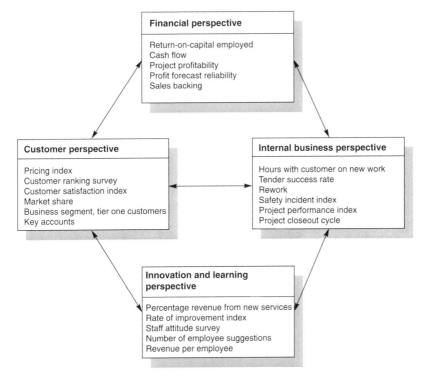

Figure 2.3 Rockwater's balanced scorecard. Reprinted by permission of *Harvard Business Review*. From 'The balanced scorecard – measures that drive performance', by Kaplan & Norton, Jan/Feb 1993. Copyright © 1993 by the President and Fellows of Harvard College, all rights reserved.

to label such measures as 'attitude surveys' is becoming increasingly misleading. More often than not the questionnaires ask for responses to one-off statements of opinion that give no real clue as to underlying attitudes. Furthermore, these opinions, so influenced by the current time and circumstances, rarely if ever give clues as to what might need to be fixed systematically in the way the organisation might need to be run.

In the turbulence presently surrounding organisations, the effective management of stakeholders is crucial. Often stakeholder management has been, and sometimes perilously still is, assumed to be a matter of commonsense, dealt with by intuition. Today, leaders of organisations are not only expected to make a profit within the rigours of the market place with respect to economics, legal issues, regulatory bodies and the like, but are expected to be socially responsible and to pay heed to the demands of key stakeholders in their businesses.

A MODEL FOR STAKEHOLDER MANAGEMENT

Satisfying the dual demands of economic performance and social responsibility is a difficult and delicate balancing act. Focus on stakeholder management can assist in harnessing the intentions and values of stakeholders to underpin the power of an organisation's strategies developed with respect to this balance.

In their paper emphasising this perspective, Savage et al. (1991) stressed that simply analysing stakeholders as 'primary' – those with official, formalised or contractual interests in the organisation, or 'secondary' – those with more diverse or indirect links which can exert influence on or be affected by the organisation, is only to begin the vital process. A more wide ranging and in depth analysis is required to enable useful strategies for managing stakeholders to be realised.

They recommended that the first analysis should be:

- The stakeholder's potential for threat.
- The stakeholder's potential for co-operation.

The factors to be considered are:

- Relationship with the organisation – does the stakeholder control key resources?
- Is the stakeholder more, or less, powerful than the organisation?
- Is the stakeholder likely to be active?
- Is it likely the stakeholder could join forces with other stakeholders in support of or in opposition to a particular activity?

Figure 2.4 analyses these factors.

From here it is possible to group stakeholders under four headings and to suggest a general strategic direction for managing each type.

- The *supportive* stakeholder. The continuing co-operation of the supportive stakeholder is more likely to be ensured by

	Increases or decreases stakeholder's potential for threat	Increases or decreases stakeholder's potential for co-operation
Stakeholder controls key resources (needed by organisation)	Increases	Increases
Stakeholder does not control key resources	Decreases	Either
Stakeholder more powerful than organisation	Increases	Either
Stakeholder as powerful as organisation	Either	Either
Stakeholder less powerful than organisation	Decreases	Increases
Stakeholder likely to take action (supportive of the organisation)	Decreases	Increases
Stakeholder likely to take non-supportive action	Increases	Decreases
Stakeholder unlikely to take any action	Decreases	Decreases
Stakeholder likely to form coalition with other stakeholders	Increases	Either
Stakeholder likely to form coalition with organisation	Decreases	Increases
Stakeholder unlikely to form any coalition	Decreases	Decreases

Figure 2.4 Factors affecting stakeholder's potentials for threat and co-operation (Savage et al, 1991). Reprinted by permission of the copyright holders, Sage Publications, Inc.

involvement in a salient aspect of the organisation's development – for example, employees can be enthused by the implementation of more participative decision making.

- The *marginal* stakeholder may be consigned to the background for most of the time, but this group, typically representing minority interests, can become powerful for good or ill when excited by specific issues, especially political/environmental considerations. Monitoring carefully the climate of opinion and predicting the likely reaction of these stakeholders should prompt the organisation to act to increase support or deflect opposition.
- The *mixed blessing* stakeholder whose potential for support and threat are equally high, such as employees with premium skills, or companies offering complementary products, is best managed through collaborative activity – closer contract negotiation with unions for example. Failure to involve this type of stakeholder easily leads to alienation of support.

Savage et al demonstrated this graphically with an extended examination of the ill-fated Eastern Airlines which struggled for two years prior to liquidation to rescue a situation made fatal by failure to assess and classify key stakeholders. Thus the ALPA (Airline Pilots' Association) moved to oppose the management's treatment of ground workers represented by the IAM (International Association of Machinists) by staging a sympathy strike – moving from mixed blessing to non-supportive stakeholder category.

Even worse, the knock-on effect impacted on other mixed blessing stakeholders like creditors and travel agents who lost faith as Eastern went into the early stages of bankruptcy. As business passengers and tour companies were left with worthless bookings, the catastrophe of formerly supportive stakeholders flipping directly into the non-supportive category compounded Eastern's ills.

- The *non-supportive* stakeholder, including powerful competitors or political masters, has a high threat potential of course, and the organisation needs to maintain its defence strategy assiduously.

From even this glancing encounter with the notion of the complex potential of stakeholder influence, it becomes clear that the overarching strategy of the organisation should be directed at changing the relationship with the stakeholder to a more favourable position.

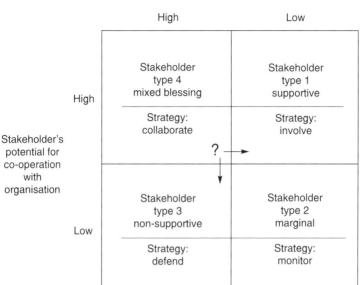

Figure 2.5 Diagnostic typology of organisational stakeholders (Savage et al, 1991). Reprinted by permission of the copyright holders, Sage Publications, Inc.

This strategy is on-going, not left to a reactive response. From corporate level to business unit to daily working practices, the management of stakeholders needs to be an integrated process, never assuming a static stakeholder position. The actions and support of stakeholders are issue-sensitive and key stakeholders should be identified with alacrity as situations develop. Savage et al leave us with a checklist for effective stakeholder management which probably merits inclusion in all our daily considerations:

- Analyse stakeholder stakes and powers.
- Identify critical dimensions of the stakeholder.
- Facilitate managers to challenge their own assumptions.
- Examine negotiations with stakeholders to improve effectiveness.
- Balance conflicting demands from equally powerful stakeholders.
- Create strategies to enhance co-operation.

UNDERSTANDING STAKEHOLDERS' NEEDS

The checklist above, at first glance, seems helpful. Its pragmatism and simplicity is compelling. However, when you look more closely, embedded in each step are many intricacies. For instance, how do you go about identifying the 'critical dimensions of each stakeholder'. The simplest and most serviceable answer to that question is 'just ask'! The work of social scientists over the last 40 years helps us to understand that 'just asking' will not do. Sometimes, indeed, asking is not sufficient. Sometimes just asking is neither reasonable nor reliable. Much of the work of business leaders is thrown into confusion by the often confounding processes of data collection for important stakeholder groups. How should we begin research into the real needs, perceptions and loyalty of our customers, our suppliers, our employees? Should we accept at face value the research mumbo jumbo of our market research or employee communication consultants? As social scientists our view is that we should be cautious about any over-enthusiasm with solutions too quickly offered.

Figure 2.6 based on the work of Galtung (1967), helps us to see that there might be creative alternatives to the immediate choice of research strategy.

Our experience suggests that all too often the confidence in data derived from informal strategies is greater than that from more systematic 'formal' methods. 'Morale is at an all-time low; I heard two employees talking about it on a bus last week,' or 'Did you see what the Lex column implied in that piece today?' or even 'We had fifty customer-complaint letters about that issue.' There is a certain resonance, a compelling sense of the truth surrounding these events in all our lives. We should not, however, be lulled into a sense of security such that these data should drive our management of our three critical stakeholders.

For instance, in our experience, there exists wide-ranging confusion in many managers' minds about the way they should collect data from their customers. The most frequently used methodologies are 'mystery-shopping'; focus groups and short 'tick-box' questionnaires, often managed and administered by market-research agencies.

FORM OF RESPONSE

SITUATION	Non-verbal	Verbal	Written
Informal	Systematic observation without participant involvement (video taping, filming mystery shopping)	Conversations, chats, gossiping, using informants; eavesdropping	Analysis of letters of complaint; newspaper articles; espionage
Formal	Experimental situations (mock up of new store or product or system design)	Formal interviews; focus groups; telephone surveys	Questionnaires; feedback forms; opinion surveys

Figure 2.6 A matrix of forms of data collection (based upon Galtung, 1967)

Figure 2.7 shows an expansion of the simple framework suggested by Galtung. In all more than 30 techniques are listed. Notice, however that there are two primary distinctions.

- First, what we call *focus*. The difference between whether we are interested in the customers' experience of the present product or service or whether we are interested in getting the customers' views as to their future needs, motivations and expectations. This distinction is vital. The research methodologies are essentially different and yield different sorts of insight and data. We prefer to call the first category *customer research*; the second we call *market-research*. This distinction is often confused, particularly by market research agencies.
- Secondly, whether we wish to understand the customer's view immediately following a service or product encounter or whether we are happy to allow time, with the ravages of memory and/or mature reflection to influence the consumer's/user's judgement. Again, the research methodologies are different and yield vastly different insights and data.

Other distinctions emerge from the matrix in Figure 2.7. The distinction inherent in oral versus written techniques, implying (though not always accurately) that the former are more qualitative, the latter more quantitative. There is also the distinction between the use of data collected from loyal, regular patrons, from occasional users, and from product or service 'defectors'.

This latter distinction made by many customer-service writers, suggests that such separations enable vital insight to be gained. There is a clear distinction to be made between these categories of customer.

- Apostles, defined as highly satisfied and completely loyal customers.
- Terrorists, defined as those customers who are mildly to extremely dissatisfied and whose loyalty is extremely suspect.
- Indifferents, those customers who fall into neither of the two previous categories.

Reichheld and Sasser (1990) estimated for instance that a 5% increase in customer loyalty can produce profit increases from 25%

	Customer experience of product or service		Customers' future wants/needs of product or service	
	Oral methods	Written methods	Oral methods	Written methods
Immediately after use of product or service	• Interviews face-to-face with customers soon after service • Interviews with customer-service personnel • Group discussions immediately after service • Mystery shopping BOX ONE	• Short, structured questionnaires soon after service completed by client/customer • Check-out satisfaction cards • Mystery shopping with structured checklist	• Depth interviews • Non-customer interviews • Focus groups • General market research interview • Structured interviews follow experience of mock-up or prototype model of product, service, environment or building • Also observation of customers of above BOX THREE	• Questionnaire follow-up following experiences of mock-up, or prototype of new products or services • Questionnaires follow-up of virtual reality experiences
Medium or long-term perspective on product or service	• Telephone interviews • Loyal customers' weekend workshops • Regular contact with loyal consumer panels • Benchmarking technology with your customers versus your competitors' customers BOX TWO	• Customer complaint analysis and tracking • Longer structured questionnaires (usually with incentives) • Service diaries • Defector follow-up by structured questionnaire • Repertory grid analysis	• Interviews with potential early-adopters, trend-setters, style gurus • Structured interviews/group discussions with service deliverers • Brainstorming with customers/non-customers about new products or service developments • Defector interviews about future needs BOX FOUR	• Delphi technology studies • Future trends analysis • Science-fiction writers; environmental, gender or sexual preference lobby or special interest groups

Figure 2.7 A more complete matrix of the methods of customer research

to 85%. Customers who are terrorists, within the zone of defection, have significant influencing power as they 'bad-mouth' a company's products or services.

Thus, data collection with a 'different' emphasis on those three categories of customers is vital for the ultimate improvement of service or product delivery.

If the 'how' of asking customers about their needs is complex so too is the 'what'.

Too often, in our experience, management leave to their professional advisers (market-research agencies usually) the range and content of what is asked of customers. The agency, acting professionally, will enquire of management whether there are specific areas or issues in which they are particularly interested or which are giving current cause for concern. These all too frequently form the core content of the enquiry process.

A more rigorous approach would seem to be either to ground the customer research in the actual concerns of the customers or to use an empirical but generalisable framework derived from substantive and authoritative research. In the former case, the research agency should base the framework of its enquiry process upon a substantial number of open-ended face-to-face interviews. These interviews should bé totally unstructured and be sufficient in number to generate the widest possible range and variety of issues. The form of the conversations should be the actual experience of being a client, consumer or customer. The sample of those interviewed should include both apostles and defectors and balance the other significant demographic variables relevant to the product or service, such as age, gender and social class.

Following these open-ended discussions, the research agency should provide management with the widest possible range of domains, factors or individual issues from which to build a comprehensive enquiry framework. It is then possible to pilot a trial run of the actual research process for further review and final agreement. Then, and only then, should the research process proper begin.

The alternative approach, that of the empirical framework, offers advantages over this essentially pragmatic and grounded assessment of the customer view of service quality. Perhaps the best known of these frameworks is that offered by Zeithaml, Parasuraman and Berry in their 1990 book *Delivering Quality Service.* These authors begin by saying that as they began their own research process, they expected to find 'a varied and rich literature that would guide us'. They say that they found nothing of the kind. Most of the literature that they did, in fact, find was about product quality, with strong advice derived from quality control principles.

They set about the task of defining a general framework that would be of value in a wide range of customer-service settings. Their research base was from four service sectors in the USA, involving telecommunications, financial services and repairs and maintenance organisations. A total of 780 customers were involved in their early research.

The research enabled the authors to develop an instrument for measuring customer's perceptions of service quality. They called the instrument SERVQUAL. In their original research, they used ten dimensions of service quality. These were derived from conversation in focus groups with customers.

The ten dimensions were:

- Tangibles: appearance of physical facilities, equipment, personnel and communication materials.
- Reliability: ability to perform the promised service dependably and accurately.
- Responsiveness: willingness to help customers and produce prompt service.
- Competence: possession of the necessary skills and knowledge.
- Courtesy: politeness, consideration and respect.
- Credibility: trustworthiness, believability and honesty.
- Security: freedom from risk or danger.
- Access: approachability and ease of access.
- Communication: keeping customers informed in language they could understand.
- Understanding the customer: making the effort to know customers and understand them.

Additional research revealed that these ten dimensions could be reduced to five factors for use in their SERVQUAL questionnaire. While tangibles, reliability and responsiveness remained distinct and separate factors, competence, courtesy, credibility and security were combined in one factor called *assurance*. Ease of access, communication and customer understanding were combined to form a new factor which Zeithaml et al labelled *empathy*. These five SERVQUAL dimensions represent the core criteria that customers, in the USA, employ in evaluating service quality. As such they might from the basis of a framework for all research into customers' needs.

However, this research was conducted in the USA using samples drawn from customers of US corporations. The present authors were mindful of the implicit differences in service experience in the United Kingdom and have conducted some research to validate these US data. Our studies, involving some 1930 customers of UK businesses in marketing telecommunications, rail transport, airlines, information management and the public service were conducted using the same ten dimensions used by Zeithaml et al. In some respects the non-US sample replicated the original factors, but there were also significant differences. Figure 2.8 show these findings.

The five factors we have derived provide an alternative framework. What we have called *professional service mastery*, the largest factor by far, implies that UK customers do not distinguish as clearly as the US sample the dimensions of reliability and responsiveness, competence and empathy. For the UK these four elements combine to form a global sense of overall service proficiency, with high expectations on all four original elements.

Additionally our sample required that service providers maintain high levels of confidentiality and security of information entrusted to them. This factor weighted more heavily than in the US research.

While presentation issues were important, the UK sample emphasised physical premises and equipment as critical, rather than the apparel of providers or the appearance of documentation.

UK respondents wanted as a discrete factor, *respect and courtesy*, including being addressed by name.

The last factor, one that we label *feedback receptiveness*, identified the need of UK customers to be asked for feedback about service provision and then to see that the feedback was acted upon. A sense that the service provider was non-defensive and open to improvement was central to this factor.

Factor label	Components	Zeithaml et al dimensions
Professional service mastery	• Proficiency in providing agreed service to high standards on-time and free from error • Proficiency in being alert, attentive and anticipating needs • Having implicit trust in the work of the service personnel, who will go the extra mile to be helpful	Reliability Responsiveness Competence Empathy
Understanding and acting with integrity	• Maintaining the confidentiality and security of information entrusted to the service personnel's safekeeping	Security
Presentation	• Maintaining premises and equipment in clean, attractive and well-maintained condition	Tangibles
Respect for me	• Maintaining courtesy and respect in the service relationship; being addressed by name	Courtesy
Feedback receptiveness	• Asking for and then acting upon customer feedback; not defensive	Understanding the customer

Figure 2.8 Five factor structure from UK customers.

THE BEST AND WORST OF UK CUSTOMER SERVICE

As a result of our research with UK customers we are able to offer some insights into the best and worst of customer service, as experienced at any rate by our sample of 1930 respondents.

The five items that scored highest in our research (a questionnaire of 53 items, using a seven-point rating scale) indicate that service providers:

- Were not deliberately dishonest.
- Were appropriately dressed.
- Were respectful.
- Were courteous and helpful on the telephone.
- Customers were often recognised by name in service interactions.

It should be noted, however, that though these items were the highest scoring, none exceeded 5.5 on a seven-point scale.

The lowest scoring items indicate that service providers:

- Rarely ask for feedback from customers about their work or seem to analyse or act upon it even when they do.
- Tend not to anticipate customer needs.
- Tend not to get things right first time.
- But also rarely seem to be having fun or acting with much energy or enthusiasm.

As this second chapter draws to a close it is worth pausing for a moment and surveying the journey we have so far undertaken. Our initial look at the external environment led us to consider three stakeholder groups and we have looked at the customer stakeholders in some detail. There can be no doubt that the issues involved in trying to understand what customers want and how this can be 'factored in' to organisational life are complex. They are not, taken altogether, difficult. In trying to find the right word to sum up this mixture of wide-ranging, complex and interacting issues the only simple word that seems to fit the bill is 'intricate'.

It is now time to move on and look at employee stakeholders. It will come as no great surprise to find that there will be intricacy here too! The employees not only have their own needs, attitudes and perceptions which will need to be taken into account, but many will also stand at organisational boundaries with other stakeholders.

Chapter Three
THE EMPLOYEE STAKEHOLDER: AN APPROACH TO MEASUREMENT

In Chapter Two we devoted much of our attention to the measurement of customers' opinions. In this chapter we will explore a way of beginning to understand the opinions, attitudes and perceptions of employees as critical stakeholders. We will focus largely upon research that we have conducted since 1989 into a measurement system which attempted to meet three often contradictory needs. The first, to build a measurement system which was scientifically defensible. The second, to provide an instrument which was both politically defensible as well as administratively convenient. The third to illuminate issues derived from employee perceptions which would promote planning and action by the driving leadership alliance.

THE INITIAL IMPETUS

The original articles by Burke and Litwin (1989 and 1992) present a dense analysis of the inter-relationships between single variables in their model. We have noted earlier the scholarly and unimpeachable quality of their work with respect to the internal dynamics of their model. One presumption, however, in their writing was not fully supported by research data. That was that the transformation variables in the model had a more potent impact upon organisation performance than those variables they labelled transactional.

Our initial research interest lay in testing this hypothesis. Was it indeed the case that these variables (leadership, vision and culture) were more likely to predict greater organisation effectiveness than variables located lower (physically) in the model? Could any research paradigm be devised which began to illuminate the truth of that proposition? Research procedures in the field of organisation performance are replete with complications and inherent inadequacy. However, we began with a modest and simple, testable question. We asked 'Do employees of high performing businesses perceive the variables in the Burke–Litwin model differently from the way employees in low-performing businesses see them?'

In order to begin our research we constructed an employee opinion survey based upon the Burke–Litwin model.

The detail of the design of the questions is not of great importance. Conventionally recognised 'good practice' was employed to build an overall questionnaire that made theoretical sense, appeared to be understandable and sensible to anyone who was asked to fill it in, would allow for data to be gathered which would be useful in themselves and which could subsequently be used to see if the component parts of the questionnaire were internally consistent.

As shown in Figure 3.1 the questionnaire was constructed of ten scales. The scales closely followed the definitions provided in the earlier Burke and Litwin papers and on research into the variables indicated in the many associated scholarly texts. The scales were:

Leadership

Ten questions which tapped employee's perceptions of the level of competence and commitment of the leadership alliance in the business. In addition the questions referred to the employee's experience of the significant *outcomes* of high quality leadership which we will detail in Chapter Four. Specifically, the extent to which they believed in the future excellence of the business and the extent to which they as an individual felt valued.

Customer service mission

Ten questions which explore the employee's perceptions of the extent of the business's responsiveness to customers. The questions

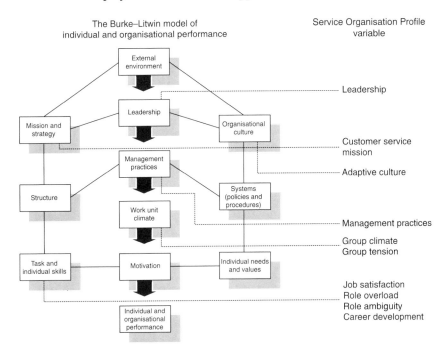

The Burke–Litwin model of individual and organisational performance

Service Organisation Profile variable

Figure 3.1 Relationship between Burke–Litwin model and Service Organisation Profile variables.

enquired about the degree to which employees believed that customers are understood, cared for and satisfied. They also included questions about the company's image among customers, and the extent to which the mission statement about customer service was clear to employees.

Adaptive culture

Twenty questions were written which enquired about the nature of the culture of the enterprise. Specifically we targeted questions in the direction of an adaptive culture. We will discuss at length in Chapter Six the specifics of such a culture. At this point we suggest that a working definition would be the extent to which employees believe that the culture of the business is proactive and that the culture allows the business to respond rapidly and effectively to changes driven by the needs of the external environment. A high score of this scale would suggest higher levels of adaptability.

Management practices

Twenty questions, four in each of five clusters, which attempted to describe some aspects of the behaviour of the employee's immediate manager or supervisor. The questions, drawn from a wide framework of possible practices, included issues associated with providing clarity and feedback about the employee's performance; about the level and nature of trust in the relationship with the supervisor; the nature of motivation and involvement employed by the manager; the extent to which the manager acted as a mentor and finally about the extent of teamwork.

Group climate

The feelings and attitudes within the work group. A high score indicated group cohesion, mutual respect and a sense of collective well-being.

Group tension

The degree of tension and conflict within the group and between the group and its management. For consistency with other dimensions where 'more is good', a high score here showed low levels of tension and conflict.

Job satisfaction

General attitudes to the employee's own job. A high score showed a positive level of job satisfaction. It should be noted, however, that this scale did not measure the employee's attitude to pay or benefits.

Role overload

The extent to which the individual saw the demands of the job as burdensome. A high score indicated that it was often difficult to cope with the demands of the job. High scores are often linked with high levels of organisational stress.

Role ambiguity

The extent to which people felt uncertain about what was expected of them. Ambiguity can arise when people are not clear of what expectations, obligations and privileges relate to their jobs. A high score showed that people were unclear about what was expected of them.

Career development

The extent to which employees believed the company recognised and fostered an individual's own career aspirations and interests.

The reader will note that two variables in the original Burke–Litwin model, systems and structure, were not included in the employee opinion questionnaire. For both practical and technical reasons we were unable to include questions about these two factors. First, asking employees' opinions about structure seemed impractical. An individual may have a view as to whether or not he/she is reporting to the most appropriate manager but it seemed less likely that a collective view as to whether the entire division or department was appropriately located would be viable. Similarly, it would seem unlikely that there would be a coherent view as to the overall structure of the entire enterprise. Despite the fact that in the UK today much organisation change is confined almost entirely to structural change (some have suggested that it is often little more than moving deckchairs on the *SS Titanic*), the overriding rule must always be 'form follows function'.

As to systems, we faced similar though perhaps more complex problems. The purpose of the questionnaire, as we have said, was primarily to examine the differences in employees' views in high performing and lower performing businesses. Many systems issues are organisation specific.

There are a vast range of systems:

- Information technology.
- Personnel policy.
- Communication.
- Financial control.

and, in any case, Burke and Litwin were unhelpful in their own definition of this factor.

The variety precluded a comprehensive and generalised list on which to ask employees to pass an opinion across a wide variety of business sectors. However, within other sections of the questionnaire, specifically within the adaptive culture, management practices, and group climate, respondents were asked to comment indirectly upon aspects of personnel policy and systems.

Thus a first draft questionnaire was ready. Following some initial 'piloting' in which the language structure of each question was checked for comprehension and the use of a seven-point scale was confirmed as suitable. All that remained was to choose a suitable name to describe the questionnaire.

WHAT'S IN A NAME?

A name for the questionnaire soon suggested itself. It was intended to help an organisation look inside itself and assess how well its employees felt it was doing in servicing the needs of its stakeholders so the word 'service' clearly had to be in there somewhere. The questionnaire was not looking at a single issue or measure, it was covering a range or set of layers which could be pictured or 'profiled' from transformational variables down to the important but potentially less potent levers of transactional factors. Thus, to christen the questionnaire as the Service Organisation Profile (SOP) may not have rated high in creativity but had the singular advantage of being robustly honest and descriptive.

A PIECE OF SERENDIPITY

No sooner had a workable version of the SOP been developed than opportunities arose to use it with immediate practical effect with two radically different businesses. One was a small hotel with an exciting reputation for customer service that was the envy of its competitors. In an environment where break even for most hotels was computed as being about two-thirds room occupancy, this hotel was regularly filling over 90% of available rooms. The need for input from an employee opinion survey was simply to make sure they were staying ahead of the pack. A second organisation had problems of a different nature. Simple good manners as much as client confidentiality make it necessary for us to avoid naming names. Let us simply say that it was a public transport organisation in a pre-privatised condition with an outstanding reputation for customer service. Unfortunately, it was outstandingly bad customer service.

These two radically different situations provided a first obvious test of our research question. An immediate test of whether the SOP did, in fact, measure significant differences would be the extent to which the scales reflected the difference between an externally recognised good provider of customer service and one that was viewed as being bad. The technically minded will recognise this as an initial opportunity to demonstrate the external validity of the SOP. In any terms the issue here was clearly that if significant differences could not be shown then the whole development of the SOP would need to be counted as an interesting speculative exercise for an armchair theoretician and one that could be quietly forgotten!

The actual differences that emerged are shown in Figure 3.2. The axes of the graph represent the scores given by employees of the two organisations on each of the ten scales that comprise the SOP. This way of presenting data from the SOP is very effective in allowing the reader's eye to scan the whole of the picture and see an overview of how an organisation (or group or individual) is being scored without losing sight of the actual size of the ratings that have been given. For ease of comparison in the charts that follow actual numerical scores are not used and the data are expressed as percentiles. As time has

THE SERVICE ORGANISATION PROFILE
A Comparison of Data for Two Companies on Ten Factors

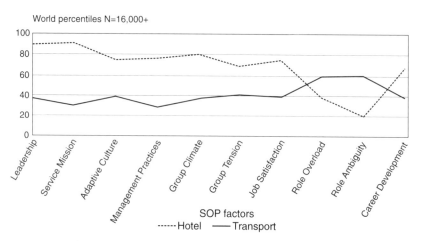

Figure 3.2 The Service Organisation Profile (SOP); a comparison of data for two service companies (hotel and transport) on ten factors.

passed since this initial study it has been possible to gather SOP data from many different organisations from all corners of the world, and some of these data are used as a norm base upon which comparisons can be made. (See Appendix I for a full worldwide list of contributing organisations.)

The figure shows the results of perceptions of the employees in each organisation to an identical questionnaire. The questionnaires were completed within six weeks of each other.

Two issues seem immediately clear from this first test of the SOP. First, the opinions of the employees differ; the magnitude of the differences seem largest at the top of the model (leadership; customer-service mission; adaptive culture; management practices) and somewhat less pronounced lower down the model (job satisfaction; career development). Second, that the two measures of 'stress' cross over. The hotel staff reported significantly lower levels of stress than the employees of the transport system.

As a first indication, the SOP seemed to provide data that were encouraging. However, some parameters of the study were weak. First, the two organisations were of vastly differing sizes. The hotel had 170 employees, each of whom contributed to the survey. The transport company had 16000 of whom 1600 randomly selected employees completed the questionnaire. In addition, the two businesses were in different industry sectors; one in hospitality, the other in transportation.

A further two studies helped refine the SOP and its application. The first attempted to control both for the number of employees and for the industry sector.

Figure 3.3 shows the results of a 10% randomly stratified sample of employees drawn from two businesses in the transport sector. Both organisations employed approximately 36000 people. The first, a railway company, was performing very badly. Over-running budgets together with an appalling record of customer service, including a poor record of punctuality; uncaring personal service;

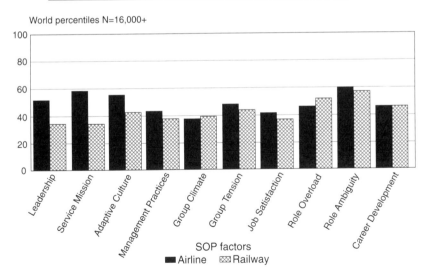

Figure 3.3 The Service Organisation Profile (SOP); A comparison of data for two service companies (airline and railway) on ten factors.

graffiti and lawlessness both in train and in waiting areas as well as continuous complaints about lack of air-conditioning and blocked and unsanitary on-train toilet facilities. The railway was exceeding its annual budget by tens of millions of dollars.

The second was an airline, operating outside of the United Kingdom. For many years this airline had been operating at a modest standard of performance. It had not been renowned for its levels of customer service. However, for the three years prior to the employee survey, it had been vigorously attempting, with some success, to improve both its financial and customer-service performance.

The results in Figure 3.3 confirm, though not so markedly, the results from our first study. However, we have now controlled, in broad terms, the major variables, which might have distorted the first set of data.

The third study, perhaps, illustrated the refined quality of the SOP best of all. The study was conducted within a distribution company. The company ran a number of distributorships within Great Britain and Northern Ireland; 120 in all. It had had, until one year before the study, a well-deserved national reputation for providing high levels of customer service. It had slipped from the number one slot to the fourth-ranking provider, according to independent industry assessments. It was anxious to understand how it might once again become number one in the customer-service league.

The study involved the six best and the six worst dealerships in the network. National corporate staff calculated an index for each dealership based upon sales volume and warranty claims as well as independent customer service evaluations. The twelve distributorships were invited to collaborate in a research study, in which the staff of each dealership completed SOP questionnaires. The results for the best six and least good six are shown in Figure 3.4.

Once again, the proposition from the Burke–Litwin model seems to be borne out. The major differences between the high performing businesses and the lower performing businesses seem to be, in the opinions of the staff of those businesses, in the variables labelled as transformational. In addition, in this case, the perception of the quality of the management practices seems also to differentiate.

THE SERVICE ORGANISATION PROFILE
A Comparison of Data for Two Groups of Dealerships

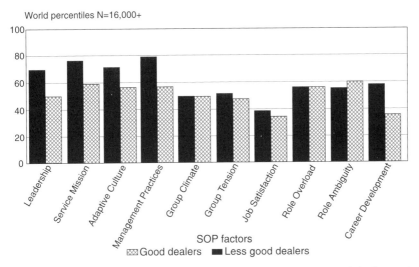

Figure 3.4 A comparison of data for two groups of dealerships (good dealers and less good dealers).

SOME NOTES ON THE SCIENTIFIC BASIS OF THE SOP

In judging the scientific basis of any scale of opinion, indeed any psychological test of any kind, we are required to answer the question 'To what extent is this instrument or test reliable?' Reliability refers here to the issue of consistency. Put simply, any individual completing a test or a questionnaire should get about the same score if he or she took the test or filled up the questionnaire twice within a short period of time, say within one week. There are three basic methods of judging the degree to which a questionnaire yields consistent measurements, each involves the use of correlational procedures. The method we used in assessing the reliability of the SOP is known as the split-half reliability co-efficient. Correlation procedures all yield a single number as a measure of reliability. The number varies between 0 and 1.00. The question is 'What does this number mean?'

Most social scientists would argue that a test reliability coefficient in the order of 0.75 or above is acceptable, with figures in the 0.90s highly desirable.

Using a sample of 16 383 respondents, drawn from some 60+ organisations, to the 95-item SOP, the split-half reliability co-efficient is calculated as 0.96. Put simply this statistic suggests that if asked to complete the questionnaire twice, say within one week, almost all respondents will give the same responses. In short the SOP is highly reliable.

When we look inside the questionnaire, into its ten constituent scales, we find split-half reliability coefficients (again for the sample of 16 000+) which range from 0.75 (for the role ambiguity factor) to 0.98 for management practices. Half of the factors (five) score in the 0.90s. Further evidence that the questionnaire will give high levels of consistency from one week to the next. The full matrix of data is shown in Appendix III.

The second critical scientific question about the SOP concerns the issue of validity. In its broadest sense validity means truth. Thus the validity of the SOP may be defined as the extent to which it pictures or represents the truth about that which it purports to measure. In the early examples shown in Figures 3.2 and 3.3, we have suggested that there were early indications of face-validity. It seemed to look right. But such sloppy language is insufficient proof.

Two further tests of this seem worthy of reporting. The first concerns the extent to which the factors in SOP mirror the relationships which Burke and Litwin suggest in their model, irrespective of the level of performance of the enterprises involved. Again using the sample of 16 000+ employees, we show the correlations between each factor in the model in Figure 3.5. With this sample size all correlations between the scales are statistically significant.

However, statistical significance is of little value here. What we are concerned with is the relative intellectual significance of the statistics.

Some observations support the Burke–Litwin model. First, the strikingly large correlations between leadership and the two other transformational variables, mission and adaptive culture (0.75 and 0.85) confirm their linking together atop the model. The looser relationship between these three variables and management

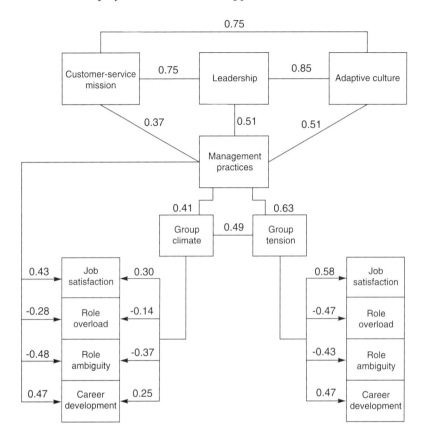

Sample size 16 383.
All correlations significant beyond 0.01 level of confidence.
Appendix III shows the full matrix.

Figure 3.5 A schematic diagram of the correlations (derived from 16,000+ respondents to the SOP).

practices seem collectively also to support the general model. It is at the transactional level of the model where there are some interesting variations. Clearly in our sample the perception of the manager's behaviour is more closely associated with the tension experienced by the group than its climate. Following the right-hand channel we see clearly more association between the perception of group tension and job satisfaction, role overload and role ambiguity, than between group climate and these variables. Our respondents could be interpreted as saying 'managers behaving badly increase group tension; group tension relates to my job satisfaction as well as to my sense of role overload and role ambiguity'. The direct relationship between management practices and the last four factors in the SOP is shown on the extreme left-hand side of Figure 3.5. For a complete matrix see Appendix III.

All in all, these data support the notion that management practices, the way managers behave on a day-to-day basis, are pivotal in any model of organisation effectiveness. Leadership is clearly not the same 'thing' as management practice. In addition if we wish to influence strongly the way people think and feel in an enterprise, we must be prepared to recognise the critical nature of these managerial practices. Thus in the Georgiades and Macdonell version of the model, we insist that the specification of the core 'dos' and 'don'ts' of managerial behaviour must first be aligned to the required vision and culture and secondly must, in that process of alignment, be specified in detail by the driving alliance of leaders.

THE SOP, CUSTOMER SERVICE AND PROFITABILITY

For some years the Harvard Business School has postulated a relationship between employee attitudes, customer satisfaction/loyalty and profitability. We first became aware of empirical evidence which supported these relationships as early in 1985. In a seminal study, Ben Schneider and David Bowen (1985) demonstrated in an unequivocal way a firm and predictable relationship between how employees in a bank felt about the way they were managed and how customers at each bank branch felt about the way they were treated as customers. The study involved more than 300 bank branches in the east coast of the USA. Branch staff whose attitudes were more positive towards their branch managers, seemed to work in branches where customers were more positive about the quality of customer service they received. The opposite was also true.

In 'Putting the service–profit chain to work' Heskett et al (1994) suggest a chain of some seven links from internal service quality through employee retention and productivity to customer loyalty and thence to revenue growth and profitability. Many links in their chain are commonsensical and require little empirical justification. Others are less clearly articulated and require at least some supporting research data.

We prefer to simplify the model and make explicit the direct relationships. We call our model the service value cycle (Figure 3.6) and it makes clear that profitability, and thus shareholder satisfaction, is driven by customer loyalty and satisfaction which is in turn driven by employee motivation, loyalty and commitment. One of the inherent problems with the Harvard position has been the lack of data (and one suspects measuring instruments) around the issue of employee attitudes. In developing the SOP our intention was clearly to build an instrument of consistency which might fill that gap.

We were able to test empirically the power of the instrument and of the service value cycle in a study of a London restaurant chain. Each of nine individual restaurants, all located in central London

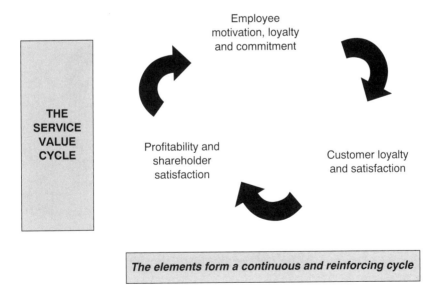

Figure 3.6 The service value cycle.

within an area of three square miles, collaborated in the study. Three sets of measures were used.

- Each member of staff in each restaurant completed the SOP. A mean score on the SOP was calculated.
- Some 830 customer interviews were conducted in the restaurants. The interviews, which were structured, took place when each customer had completed their final course, and were awaiting coffee. Each interview lasted approximately 12 minutes, and consisted of some 50 questions. One question from the interview, 'How was your meal with us today? Please rate on this seven-point scale' was used as a criterion across each restaurant. A restaurant mean score was calculated.
- Thirdly the average profit per employee was calculated for each restaurant. Net profit for the 3 months prior to the study and the 3 months post study were divided by the total number of staff employed in each restaurant during the period.

The results on each measure were submitted to a correlation test of association (the Spearman rank-order correlation coefficient). The results of the tests are shown in Figure 3.7. What the study shows is

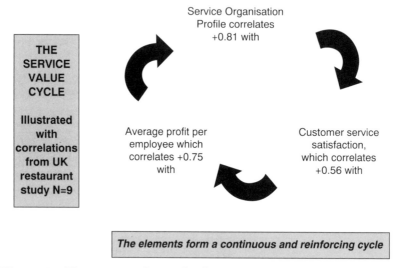

Figure 3.7 The service value cycle illustrated with correlations from UK restaurant study.

that, in broad terms, the service value cycle holds. Employee attitudes (as measured by the SOP) correlate with customer satisfaction levels +0.81. In short, 'You really cannot treat your customers better than you treat your folks.' The correlation is highly significant. Similarly, the relationships between employee attitudes and profitability is very strong. In Figure 3.8 we show the extent of that correlation of +0.75 by plotting each restaurant on the two dimensions. We claim in this study no more than Schneider and Bowen illustrated in 1985. The difference is only that the research was completed in the UK and in a different industry sector.

What we have shown is that there was a significant relationship between how employees felt about the way they were managed and how customers of each restaurant felt about the way they were treated as customers. In addition we were able to show the positive relationship between both these factors and profitability.

Over the years since its original formulation, as we have indicated, more than 30000 people and some 60 organisations have

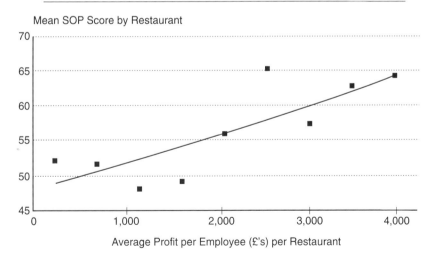

Figure 3.8 Service Organisation Profile: a plot of nine restaurants by SOP and average profit per employee.

SOP and CUSTOMER SERVICE
Average SOP Scores for Four Levels of Customer Service

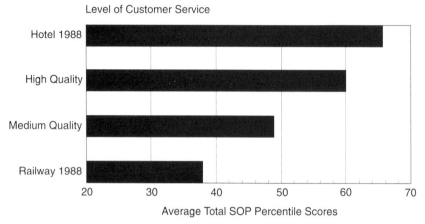

Figure 3.9 Service Organisation Profile and customer service: average SOP scores for four levels of customer service.

contributed to the development of the SOP. Because of the wide-ranging scope of the development work, we can now postulate a clear relationship between scores on the SOP and overall general levels of customer service. In Figure 3.9 we show what we believe is a supportable relationship. We illustrate the two extremes by using data from the original study. The figure suggests that overall scores on the SOP need to be in excess of the 60th percentile before an organisation will be delivering the highest possible levels of customer service.

It has been the main objective of this chapter to explain the importance of understanding the opinions, attitudes and perceptions of employees as critical stakeholders. We have also shown that these perceptions can be measured in a way that provides direct action-orientated feedback to the driving leadership alliance. We will now turn to examine the transformational variables in some depth. The next four chapters will look at leadership, vision, adaptive culture, and management practices.

Chapter Four
LEADERSHIP: THE DREAMERS OF THE DAY

AN INTRODUCTION

> All men dream; but not equally.
> Those who dream by night in the dusty
>   recesses of their minds
> Awake to find that it was vanity;
> But the dreamers of day are dangerous men,
> That they may act their dreams with open
>   eyes to make it possible.
>
> T. E. Lawrence
> *Seven Pillars of Wisdom*, Ch. 1

Few topics studied by behavioural scientists have as much relevance to society as leadership. Most people assume that the effective functioning of any social system from a junior school to a global corporation depends on the quality of leadership. That is why we blame a football manager for a losing streak or give a general the credit for a military victory.

Lieutenant General William P. Pagonis led the 40 000 people who ran the theatre logistics for the Gulf War. By any standards, the task he faced was challenging. His organisation grew from just 5 people to 40 000; they supported half a million people, distributed 7 million tons of supplies and achieved many other staggering statistics in a harsh environment with almost no pre-existing infrastructure.

Much of that success, he believed, can be attributed to qualities of leadership that the army had developed and, in an article entitled 'The work of the leader', he described those leadership principles (Pagonis, 1992). The article could almost serve as an introduction to this chapter because Pagonis makes reference to many of the important findings of leadership studies carried out this century.

He recalled his first leadership experience as a newsboy; leading the pack, but still showing empathy for the needs of younger newsboys. In his army career, he explained how his leadership skills had been developed through experience, training and a continuing will to learn. He illustrated the power of language to rally his staff behind him to achieve superhuman tasks. Most of all, he showed how leaders needed to give their staff a mission and the power to carry it out.

Pagonis was not a management theorist who was interested in leadership history. He was a practising manager in a crisis situation. His experiences show that theory is important and it can be put to practical use, even when the manager is not aware of the theory!

Although we all agree on its importance, we have to recognise that the study of leadership is a rich tapestry of sometimes conflicting theories, a conflict that is well satirised in this quotation.

> As we survey the path that leadership theory has taken, we spot the wreckage of 'trait theory'; the 'great man' theory; the 'situationist critique'; leadership styles; functional leadership, and finally, leader-less leadership; to say nothing of bureaucratic leadership, charismatic leadership, democratic-autocratic–laissez-faire leadership, group-centered leadership, reality-centered leadership, leadership by objective and so on. The dialectic and reversals of emphases in this area very nearly rival the tortuous twists and turns of child-rearing practices, and one can paraphrase Gertrude Stein by saying, 'a leader is a follower is a leader'.
>
> (Bennis, 1959)

Woody Allen catches the mood, perhaps more succinctly:

> More than any other time in history, mankind faces a crossroad. One path leads to despair and utter hopelessness; the other to total extinction. Let us pray we have the wisdom to choose correctly.

WHY DOES THIS LEADERSHIP MATTER?

Let's consider an overview of that leadership debate and try to demonstrate why it is important. While it seems that any discussion of the subject tends to be based on the assumption that we all share some common beliefs about leadership, the one single theme that runs throughout is that there are no such common beliefs. The development of the debate and the state of the debate at a given moment in time demonstrate, beyond doubt, that we do not have a common perception of leadership. We also find that not everyone agrees that leadership is important.

Some observers claim that we have spent too much time studying the activity and potential impact of a small percentage of a business community. Those same observers argue that energy and resources would be better spent at other points in the organisation, on front-line management, for example, or on those who have the most direct contact with the customer.

Despite the intensity of the debate, we believe that leadership is a vital issue. We would argue that now, more than ever, we need a clear model of what leadership is. We have reached a stage in human evolution that is characterised by change, not only the extent of change, but also its speed and potential implications.

> The greatest need for leadership is in the dark . . . It is when the system is changing so rapidly . . . the old prescriptions and old wisdoms can only lead to catastrophe, and leadership is necessary to call people to the very strangeness of the new world that is being born.
>
> (Boulding, 1985)

KEY QUESTIONS ABOUT LEADERSHIP

We have shown that there are many conflicting theories of leadership, but we also see some common ground. The answers may be very different, but the questions are often similar. The nature of these questions in themselves explains why we think leadership matters:

- What is a leader?
- What do leaders do?
- How can we identify them?
- Can we select them from their contemporaries at an early stage?

- Is it possible to develop leaders?
- Can we train people to be leaders, or are they just born?
- How should we use leaders?
- Is there more than one type of leader?
- Do we need leaders at all and, if so, when?

The key to all these questions is that, while an academic discussion might be interesting, we need to be driven by a more pragmatic approach. Any study of leadership must leave us with something we can use in the real world. Addressing those questions must help those of us who are trying to improve organisational effectiveness.

REACHING TOWARDS A DEFINITION OF LEADERSHIP

We all use the word leadership, and therefore tend to assume that we share a common definition and understanding of what it might be. Participants on leadership training courses, when asked to define leadership qualities, produce lists that regularly include terms such as vision, empathy, clarity and intelligence, yet it is a fact that, even within a single organisation, a group of managers will be unlikely to agree on one single characteristic that distinguishes a leader.

In the light of such diversity, it is not difficult to come to the conclusion that our images of leadership are entirely personal. When we are asked to describe leaders, we tend to think of examples from our own experience, or from history. We recall one or more personalities and list their outstanding characteristics.

Yet, despite these differences, it is vital that we reach a method of understanding and agreeing the characteristics of leadership because our model (Figure 4.1) suggests it is central to the effective functioning of organisations.

By inference the model suggests the centrality of leadership to the transformation process. Further, whatever else leadership may be concerned with, the model points to three central topics within the leadership task. The establishment of vision, the alignment of culture and the specification of management practices. Each of these topics will be dealt with in later chapters.

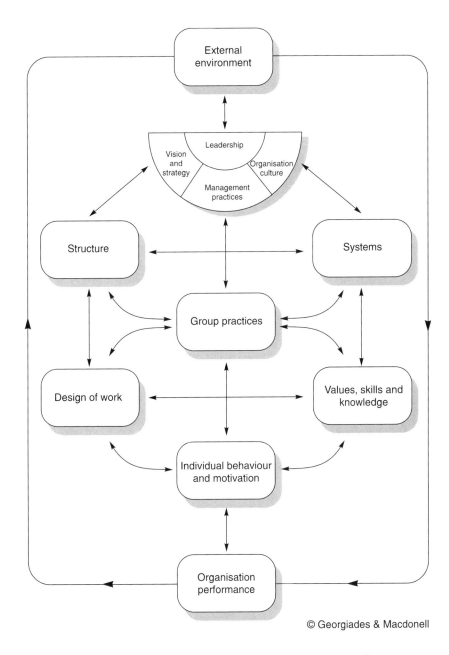

Figure 4.1 The Georgiades and Macdonell model of organisation effectiveness.

As a first step in dealing with leadership, we need to understand two facts:

- Our understanding of leadership has evolved over time, but it has not been a simple evolution. There have been significant landmarks in that evolution – some of them amplifications of previous theories, but a few representing paradigm shifts in comprehension. All of those theories have been based on considerable research and, to understand leadership now, we need to understand how it has evolved.
- The definition of leadership that we adopt must be understood by everyone. We should all commit to understanding what that definition means in terms of our own behaviour.

FROM GREAT MAN THEORY TO TRAIT THEORY

Great Man Theory

The earliest and simplest view of leadership can be called the 'great man' approach. The approach is aptly named since it assumed that men and women who displayed great vision, personality and competence rose to prominence and influenced the course of history. Alexander the Great, Julius Caesar, Joan of Arc, and Winston Churchill are popular examples of historical figures who fall into this category.

The view of leadership evolved largely through the work of historical biographers who concentrated on a limited number of characteristics that distinguished great people, for example, physical appearance, family background and achievements.

Supporters of this approach also point out that great men and women can be found recurring in certain families with unusual frequency. They point to possible genetic explanations for this. In the twentieth century, for instance, the Kennedy family is often cited as an example.

If we look at the value of great man theory in relation to issues of leadership in organisations, it has four major drawbacks:

- It encourages nepotism. If we accept the argument that leadership ability is inherited, favouritism in promotions is bound to occur as relatives of previously successful leaders enter the organisation. Currently, there is a definite bias against this method of promotion.

- It creates selection problems. If we accept the theory that leaders are born, not made, we would need to staff our organisations with born leaders. Given our present knowledge about leadership, it is simply not possible to do this.
- It devalues management development programmes. Organisations who accept the great man theory will place little emphasis on management development programmes – if leaders are born, there is no need to develop them. Equally, supporters of the theory argue, it is pointless trying to develop 'nonleaders'. However, this is an unreasonable view of the human learning process and experience shows that most managers benefit from development programmes.
- It discourages flexibility. If the great man theory is accepted, organisations will not attempt to adapt job functions/job specifications to individual managers. The great man theory assumes that true leaders will be able to analyse any situation and cope effectively with it.

Although the great man theory is an interesting approach to leadership, the in-depth analysis of a handful of prominent individuals does not give us a systematic insight into what is generally required for leadership success. The other weakness of the approach is that it has tended to concentrate on political and military figures. Now, while political and military leaders undoubtedly have a major impact on world history, many other individuals, including business leaders such as Sir John Harvey-Jones or Sir Colin Marshall, have also made a significant contribution.

TRAIT THEORY

Summary

In 1974, R. Stogdill, in his book *Handbook of Leadership*, summarised all the trait theory research from 1914 to 1973.

He concluded that the average leader tends to be superior to the average follower in the following ways:

- Intelligence (but not significantly so).
- Levels of achievement and knowledge (this does not necessarily mean education, although there is a strong correlation).
- Dependability in exercising responsibility (leaders take tasks more seriously and they demonstrate a sense of personal responsibility).
- Activity level (leaders tend to have the stamina to go on longer without fatigue).
- A capacity to promote the involvement of other people.
- A slightly higher socio-economic status (although it is impossible to tell whether this is a condition or a consequence of success).
- A greater sense of fun and use of humour!

By 1974, this was really all we knew, but the development of the trait theory had moved forward, for as Stogdill says:

> A person does not become a leader by virtue of the possession of some combination of traits, but the pattern of personal characteristics must bear some relevant relationship to the characteristics, activities and goals of the followers.

In other words, possessing the best combination of traits is not sufficient in itself. Unless these traits are relevant to the needs of the followers, the leader will not prove to be a success. Leadership requires more than just personal characteristics; it must be externally orientated. The research has moved on to the next stage and is becoming more intelligible and constructive.

The Value of Trait Theory

There are many conceptual and methodological problems with the trait theory approach to leadership. We are not saying that there are no traits associated with successful leaders, but we do feel that past research has been unable to identify those traits consistently.

So, if little evidence supports the trait theory of leadership, why are we devoting so much space to it? The fact is that, despite its poor scientific validity, it is probably the most frequently used method of identifying leaders. Many managers believe they can identify a good leader after a 15 minute conversation, by testing the firmness of a handshake, or by analysing eye contact, or the colour of their tie. It is, therefore, important to examine the conceptual and methodological problems associated with the trait theory so that we can evaluate more critically the 'armchair psychology' approach to identifying leaders.

Problems with Trait Theory

- *Similar traits in leaders and followers.* It is a fact that many people who fail as leaders, or who never achieve positions of leadership, often possess some of the same traits as successful leaders. For example, although taller people may generally be more successful as leaders, many tall people have neither the inclination nor the capability to be leaders. What's more, history shows that many short people have risen to positions of leadership.

- *Dependence on physical and psychological factors.* Both of these types of attribute have been considered traits. While physical attributes (such as height, weight or appearance) can be observed, psychological attributes (such as perseverance, intelligence or initiative) cannot technically be measured. For example, if an employee doggedly pursues a certain course of action, what trait is causing the action? Should it be called 'perseverance' or 'obsession'? Since psychological attributes cannot be measured, their existence can only be inferred from behaviour and this can lead to questionable conclusions.

- *Value judgements.* The traits possessed by successful leaders are inevitably value judged as positive. A leader is seen as decisive, strong, intelligent and persevering rather than someone who leaps to conclusions and is brutal, eggheaded and obsessed. This reluctance to admit that leaders often demonstrate negative qualities may have hindered the development of an accurate portrayal of effective leaders. One study of informal leaders in a prison, for example, showed that they tended to be homosexual, neurotic and psychopathic – hardly the values traditionally associated with leaders.

- *Varying definitions.* There appears to be little consensus on the terms used to describe traits. Stryker (1958), in a study of executive leadership qualities, demonstrated the magnitude of the problem when he asked 75 senior executives to define the term 'dependability' – a trait that regularly appears in leadership studies. The executives defined this trait in 147 different ways! Even after similar definitions had been combined, 25 different definitions remained. This lack of consensus is worrying because it makes further research into the importance of the trait very difficult.

- *Difficulties in measuring traits.* Intelligence, for example, as measured by IQ tests, is often cited as a trait of successful leaders, but there continues to be a debate about what exactly IQ tests measure. The claim that IQ tests are inherently biased against minority groups further complicates the measurement problem, since many minority group leaders are extremely effective. Even if a positive correlation between intelligence and leadership can be demonstrated, this may not prove anything. If a company uses the results of intelligence tests to promote people and a researcher finds a positive correlation between intelligence and management level, all this proves is that the company has certain promotion criteria. It does not prove that intelligence is a prerequisite for leadership.

- *Thresholds for success.* Even if a trait can be clearly defined and accurately measured, it is unclear how high a score a person must achieve to be effective. It seems logical to assume that there is a threshold, but there is little in the way of firm evidence. For example, if a person scores 8 on a 10-point scale that measures dependability, is that sufficient?

- *Role-playing.* When researchers observe the behaviour of an executive and make deductions about the traits that lay behind that behaviour, they overlook the fact that executives often behave in a manner they believe is appropriate to the job, not in a way that is consistent with their true nature. The result is that the researcher ascribes traits that the executive does not really possess and this, in turn, can lead to faulty conclusions about the traits that are necessary for effective leadership.

- *Ignoring the followers*. The fundamental assumption that leaders must have certain traits to be leaders may be incorrect. In fact, the population may need a leader and may follow anyone who is perceived as having leadership qualities. If this argument is correct, our research should focus on the followers, rather than the leaders.
- *Environment and leadership*. The trait theory assumes implicitly that leadership success is determined by qualities internal to the leader, and assumes that the leadership environment is not important. This is a very questionable assumption because environmental characteristics have an impact on leadership effectiveness. The research and theory presented in the next section indicate the importance of these environmental characteristics.

Summary

These comments do not mean that the trait theory is completely invalid. As Stogdill observed:

> . . . the view that leadership is entirely situational in origin and that no personal characteristics are predictive of leadership . . . seems to overemphasise the situational, and underemphasise the personal, nature of leadership.

It is easy to understand why trait theory developed. The belief that certain traits could be used to predict leadership effectiveness was an intuitively simple, plausible approach. Had it yielded firm evidence that specific traits predicted successful leadership, a major benefit would have resulted from a very simple idea.

It may be true that a certain group of traits exist which contribute to successful leadership, but current measurement problems prevent us identifying such a list. As our measurement tools become more powerful, we may be able to develop that list, but, in the meantime, we have to conclude that the trait theory lacks value, except in a few narrowly defined situations. Those situations are too specific to be of value to most managers.

TOWARDS A LEADERSHIP STYLE

Introduction

Although trait theory was still being studied in the 1970s, it was not the only direction for leadership research. In the 1950s, a group of research workers at Ohio State University and the University of Michigan pushed leadership studies in an entirely new direction. They decided to stop searching for those inherent traits; instead, they set themselves three goals. First, to discover what leaders actually did; second, to find out what effect the leaders' behaviour had on employee satisfaction and performance; and, third, to identify a best leadership style.

Two other pieces of work followed the general lines set by the Ohio and Michigan studies. Blake and Mouton (1976) in '*The New Managerial Grid*' sought to help managers identify their current leadership style and then develop the single most appropriate style. Hersey and Blanchard (1972) took this a stage further and sought to demonstrate how a flexible leadership style could be adapted to the development level of different groups of subordinates, providing effective leadership, whatever the situation.

The Ohio Studies

J. K. Hemphill, leader of the Ohio studies, published his findings in a book entitled *The Leader Behavior Description* (1950). Ohio researchers found that leaders and managers have two important characteristics:

- Consideration for the follower (or follower-orientated behaviour). Leaders recognise that people have needs and goals and seek recognition for their achievements.
- Initiation of structure. Leaders communicate what they expect of their people and what their people can expect from the leader.

These two characteristics interact directly to influence the performance and satisfaction of workgroups and most leaders demonstrate both characteristics to a degree. In essence, the researchers argue that all you have to do to be a good manager is to tell your team what to do and take care of them while they are doing it. This is not difficult to understand; yet, as managers, we probably don't do it very often.

The Michigan Studies

The Michigan studies were almost contemporary with the Ohio studies and resulted in some very similar conclusions. After studying numerous industrial situations, Kahn and Katz (1960) concluded that two leadership styles influenced employee performance and satisfaction:

- Employee-centred leaders who were interested in their subordinates as people. They showed concern for their welfare and encouraged workers to get involved in goal setting.
- Production-centred leaders who emphasised the technical aspect of the job, set work standards and closely supervised their workers.

The best known of the Michigan studies was conducted in a large insurance company where a field experiment was designed to test the impact of employee-centred and production-centred leadership on the output of four divisions of the company. The researchers found that:

- Productivity increased under both leadership styles (20% under employee-centred, 25% under production-centred).
- Employee satisfaction and turnover were adversely affected by production-centred leadership.

The Michigan researchers drew some general conclusions from their findings:

- Employee-centred leaders supervised groups with higher productivity and morale.
- Production-centred leaders supervised groups with lower productivity and morale.
- Employee-centred leadership was therefore thought to be superior to production-centred leadership.

Conclusion

The conclusions of the Michigan group are very similar to the Ohio findings and both have been valuable in identifying specific leadership behaviours that influence employee productivity and satisfaction. However, there has been no clear evidence that any one style of leadership is always effective. When attempts were made to apply either set of ideas into the world of work the differing results emphasised the importance of environmental rather than purely behavioural variables.

The New Managerial Grid

The application of the original Ohio and Michigan work can be seen with greatest clarity in the development by Blake and Mouton of what came to be called the new managerial grid (Blake and Mouton, 1976). They designed an organisation development programme that emphasised the two basic leadership behaviours of concern for people and concern for production, identified by the earlier researchers. Blake and Mouton assumed that these two concerns are independent, increased and decreased concerns for production and people can occur simultaneously. They set these dimensions at right angles, identified nine points of measurement from 1 being low to 9 being high for each, thus giving an overall potential set of 81 possible styles that could be plotted on the grid. Of these, five have been most frequently described and used as benchmarks:

The 1.1 style   *Impoverished management.* No real concern for either production or people.

The 5.5 style   *Balancing* both sets of concerns to 'satisfy' what gets done rather than taking risks to push or emphasise either.

The 9.9 style   *Team management.* Commitment to both people and a common purpose which leads to trust and respect.

These three are in ascending order of assumed 'goodness'. The two other styles offered as descriptive benchmarks are the two where one high concern is balanced with one that is low:

The 1.9 style   *Country club*, where attending to the needs of the people is all important.

The 9.1 style   *Authority–obedience*, where efficiency comes from so arranging work that human elements have a minimum of possible interference.

This model was designed to help managers first identify their current leadership style and then help them develop the most appropriate style. According to Blake and Mouton, the most desirable style is 9.9, where managers show a similar concern for both people and production, but this has not been a view shared by everyone. Compare this with a contrary view held by two other researchers, Bernardin and Alvares (1976):

> Despite the abundance of contrary evidence, Blake and Mouton asserted that their 9.9 team manager, high on production and high on people, will always be the most effective type of leader regardless of the situation and, in fact, a 9.9 orientation applied to the organisation as a whole will foster a kind of corporate Darwinism.

The belief that there is one leadership style that is inherently superior to others is clearly contrary to a contingency idea of leadership. It seems unlikely that the 9.9 management style is appropriate for organisations experiencing different growth rates, labour relations, competition, and a host of other differentiating problems. In the next section we will examine contingency theories of leadership.

Situational Leadership

The need to balance almost any approach to leadership against the prevailing circumstances led almost inevitably in the direction of so-called 'contingency theories' – so called because the idea behind the word 'contingency' is simply one of saying 'it all depends . . .'. There was, however, a sense of agreement amongst thinkers on the nature of leadership in the late 1960s and 1970s that the 'what it all depended upon' was the situation in which the leader had to behave.

Fiedler (1967) was perhaps the first and most influential proponent of the situational approach. His use of a seemingly simple personality test for leaders had echoes of our earlier comments about trait theorists but he concluded, again from studies largely within military contexts, that there were three important aspects of situations that would influence leadership effectiveness:

- Leader–member relationships. Leaders who are liked and respected have real power and do not need to use rank or status.
- Task structure. Highly structured tasks give immediate feedback when instructions are not being followed and corrective action can be quickly taken. 'Loose' tasks do not allow precise action and quick sanctions.
- Position power. The authority carried by the leader by virtue of his or her position to impose rewards and sanctions.

In a not dissimilar vein, House described the path–goal theory in 1971 by developing the theme that leader behaviour should be motivating to subordinates by smoothing their path towards personal satisfaction and payoffs by removing the obstacle, pitfalls and roadblocks that stood in the way.

House identified four categories of leader behaviour that would influence motivation:

- Instrumental or 'directive' leadership. Making tasks clear, showing how they can be carried out, what each subordinate's role is in the process, and so on.
- Supportive leadership. Being friendly and supporting a subordinate's wellbeing and status.
- Participative leadership. Involving and consulting subordinates.
- Achievement-oriented leadership. Setting high standards and encouraging subordinates to aspire to achieving taxing and lofty goals.

From these there are clearly three sets of situational factors that need to be considered:

- The task.
- The characteristics of subordinates.
- The nature of the subordinate group.

Unfortunately, these simple ideas turned out to give rise to so many different leadership styles and situational factors that just as with Fiedler's list of contingencies the practising manager is left more than a little in the dark to know how to apply these seemingly simple and interesting ideas in practice.

Vroom and Yetton (1973) seemed to be addressing this problem when they laid out a set of prescriptions intended to help leaders select an appropriate style. Hersey and Blanchard (1972) looked at the transactions between leaders and followers in terms of how far the psychological maturity and job experience should be the main factors (prime contingencies) affecting the decisions a leader should make.

All these models which emphasise situational aspects had some initial success and hope for ever-wider application, but all seemed to run into difficulty when trying to escape from the laboratory into the 'real world' of what leaders and followers actually did. All these approaches did, as Bass and Stogdill (1990) pointed out, advance our understanding about how leadership must fit into an ex-ternal context. The ideas outlined above share an acknowledgement that:

- There is a leadership spectrum with task orientation at one end and relationship orientation at the other.
- Task-orientated leaders have a high concern for goals. They often have a high 'need to achieve', in the sense of needing measurable external indicators of how well they have performed, are frequently hard-driving persuaders, are often aloof, autocratic and seen as controllers.
- Relationship-orientated leaders have a high concern for group maintenance, focusing on support affiliation, interaction and social ties.

Bass and Stogdill also identified two other types of leader who do not fall into the task–relationship orientation. Those who drift from one mediocre performance to another until removed from the leader role, and those he called 'switch-hitters'. These are benevolent autocrats who are sufficiently enlightened to encourage participation in decision making, even if this goes a little against the grain, because it ultimately helps to achieve better performance.

Conclusion

By the early 1980s the waves of enthusiasm that encouraged researchers to move from trait to behaviour-based and then to situational approaches to leadership seemed to lose their impetus. Empirical research was just not offering anything other than general and superficial insights into leadership. The mode was almost one of pessimism. There was a wall of inconsistent findings and methodological problems that no one idea or approach could seem to surmount. There was clearly a need for a radical appraisal and some new thinking about leadership.

A PARADIGM SHIFT

Introduction

In the previous section, we looked at the way researchers were trying to identify 'best' leadership styles. They did this by considering two important characteristics of leaders; how well they take care of their followers and how well they tell them what to do. However, by concentrating on those two characteristics, the researchers developed only a limited view.

The next two sets of studies looked at what managers and leaders actually do. In the course of their work, the researchers identified many other characteristics that contribute to successful leadership.

The first series of studies inspired originally by the work of Henry Mintzberg, observed many different managers and reached ten broad conclusions about their work. McCall and Lombardo also studied groups of managers and leaders, but they sought to identify those characteristics that differentiated successful from 'derailed' leaders.

The Work of Henry Mintzberg

At this point, there was a fundamental shift. We have moved through great man theory and trait theory to theories dependent on team needs. Henry Mintzberg, while working at New York University, initiated a new research perspective (Mintzberg, 1973). He decided to look at what managers actually do. Although this sounds like a relatively simple concept, it was a paradigm shift in the leadership research.

Mintzberg and his followers used three principal research techniques:

- Managers were asked to keep a diary for a month and list all their activities. They were issued with a timer and, every 15 minutes, they would stop and write down what they were currently doing. This proved to be a burden, but it did produce some useful data.
- A research worker was assigned to each manager to make notes about the activities. This was still not completely satisfactory.
- Managers were connected to microphones. All verbal communications were recorded and, if managers were writing, they simply stated aloud what they were doing.

Now, for the first time, researchers were able to describe definitively what managers actually do.

We may summarise the findings from a series of 25 research studies using the research tools listed above (McCall et al, 1978). Many of these findings are obvious and most are recognisable from our own experience. The findings can be summarised in ten broad statements about a manager's work:

- *Managers work long hours.* The researchers found that the average manager was working between 50 and 90 hours a week. Evenings are taken up with paperwork, preparation for meetings and work-related social events. The total number of hours varies with rank and functional responsibility.
- *Managers are busy.* A number of the studies show that managers demonstrate a high average level of activities during the day. Typically, a manager will deal with 100 to 200 different incidents, activities or episodes during an eight-hour day. An average supervisor will have more than double this number of inter-actions.
- *Managers have to make decisions quickly.* The researchers found that managers typically spend between five and seven minutes on a

given task. Their day is characterised by interruptions and discontinuity. Senior executives reported that only 10% of their activities lasted an hour or more, while a quarter of their activities lasted less than nine minutes.

- *A manager's job is varied.* A typical day might include dealing with thirty-six pieces of paper, four scheduled and four unscheduled meetings, five telephone calls and one tour. A high proportion of the day is spent in contact with a wide variety of people.
- *Managers are homebodies.* Although managers claim to practise visible management and walk the shop, the researchers found that most managers spend the majority of time in their own office.
- *Managers' work is primarily oral.* The studies showed that managers at higher level spend up to 90% of their time talking to other people – the average is around 65 to 70%.
- *Managers use a lot of contacts.* The average manager spends 26 to 30% of the day with subordinates. At a senior level, the figure can be higher with half to two-thirds of the time in contact. At lower supervisory levels, the figure is about one-third to one-quarter.
- *Managers do not spend much time on planning.* The researchers concluded that it was difficult, with only seven minutes per task, to plan effectively.
- *Information is the basic ingredient of managers' work.* The studies found that managers spend 25 to 50% of their time getting information. However, that information may not be used for the key decision-making process, which only accounts for 8 to 13% of a manager's time.
- *Managers don't know how they spend their time.* Research confirmed that managers believe they spend more time on important activities than they actually do. They overestimated the time spent on phone calls, reading and production, while underestimating the time spent on meetings and informal contacts.

Summary

These results seem to contradict the claims of earlier researchers. Apparently, managers are so bound up in day-to-day problem-solving that managing their people seems to be an unlikely event. As a result, managers tend to engage in what many would regard as 'shooting from the hip' when dealing with the needs of the people who work for them.

Succession and the Derailed Executive

Morgan McCall and Michael Lombardo (1983), working at the influential Center for Creative Leadership in North Carolina, continued the process of observing managers and leaders at work. They were trying to find out, not just what managers and leaders do, but what were the differences between successful and 'derailed' leaders.

They conducted research by interviewing senior executives in three US-based industrial organisations. They wanted to find out why some executives were successful and some derailed, by talking to the senior executives, to their colleagues and to their subordinates.

They found many similarities between executives who succeeded and those who derailed. Both groups were:

- Extremely bright.
- Identified early in their careers.
- Had outstanding track records.
- Had very few flaws.
- Ambitious.
- Had made many sacrifices.

The successful executives shared a number of characteristics:

- They had more jobs during their careers, either in the same or in different organisations.
- They had experience in a variety of roles.
- They maintained composure under stress and they handled mistakes with poise.
- When they had problems, they focused on them and solved them.
- They got along with all sorts of different people.
- They were outspoken without being offensive.

McCall and Lombardo also discovered that executives who derailed shared at least two of the following characteristics:

- Specific performance problems with the business; for example, they didn't make profit targets, couldn't handle certain jobs or failed to change.
- Insensitivity to other people, exhibiting an abrasive, bullying or intimidating style.
- Cold, aloof or arrogant, which made them difficult to work with.
- Betrayed trust and did not keep their promises.
- Failed to delegate or build a team around them.
- Over-ambitious; constantly looking for the next job.
- Failed to staff effectively; they picked the wrong people or chose someone in their own image.
- Unable to think strategically; they could never get away from attention to detail.
- Unable to adapt to a boss with a different style.

Failure Points

McCall and Lombardo believe that both successful and derailed executives had plenty of flaws, but these were only exposed in certain circumstances when:

- They lost a boss who had covered their weaknesses.
- They entered a job for which they were ill prepared.
- They left a trail of small problems or injured people which eventually caught up.
- They were not scrutinised during promotion until it was too late.
- They entered the executive suite where they had to get on with other people.

The authors concluded at that time that no executive could possess all of the skills required for success. Executives were a patchwork of strengths and weaknesses and, on that basis, there was no foolproof guarantee that they would succeed or fail.

Recent Findings

A later study, using similar methodology, by Morrison, White and Van Velsor in 1987 broadly confirmed these findings amongst women 'derailers'. A further study, this time with a much enhanced sample of men and women by Lombardo and McCauley in 1988 replicated both earlier sets of findings. However, all three of these early studies were conducted in US companies. In 1995 the *Academy of Management Executive* reported the work of Van Velsor and Leslie who studied executives in both 15 US-based *Fortune* 500 companies and 24 large companies in Belgium, Germany, France, Italy, the United Kingdom and Spain. Four enduring themes emerged:

- Problems with interpersonal relationships (reported twice as frequently amongst European managers than US managers as derailment causes).
- Failure to meet business objectives (despite early initial, often out-standing, success).
- Inability to build and lead a team (25% in European cases; 20% in US cases).
- Inability to change and adapt during transition (almost two-thirds of both samples derailed for these reasons).

Despite the minor differences noted above, Van Velsor and Leslie concluded that the dynamics of derailment do not differ dramatically between the US and European companies they studied.

Conclusion

Both of the studies in this section give us the opportunity to observe real managers and leaders at work, to find out what they do and to analyse why they succeed or fail. Both studies demonstrate that two of the most important requirements of a successful leader or manager are interpersonal competence and oral competence. The Mintzberg studies highlighted the high percentage of time managers spent working with other people and showed that each of the contacts was likely to last for just a short time. He also showed that the majority of a manager's work is oral. These findings suggest that interpersonal and oral skills must be well developed for success and this appears to be confirmed by the work of McCall and Lombardo who cited interpersonal and oral incompetence to be a strong cause of executive failure.

MANAGERS AND LEADERS ARE DIFFERENT

Introduction

Up to this point, researchers have assumed that leaders and managers share the same characteristics and succeed or fail for the same reasons. The work of Mintzberg and McCall and Lombardo has given us a clearer picture of what managers and leaders actually do, and they have highlighted oral and interpersonal skills as an area for possible management development. However, the two studies in this section take the debate in an entirely new direction. Zaleznik and, later, Burns contend that managers and leaders are different. Because they are different and because they play different roles, the authors argue that organisations must recognise the difference and plan their management development programme accordingly.

The Work of Zaleznik

Abraham Zaleznik added something very special to the leadership debate by making one of those intuitive leaps that is rare in the history of leadership research. In 1977, he published an article in the *Harvard Business Review* entitled, 'Managers and leaders: are they different?' In the article, Zaleznik stated that we need to recognise that there really is a difference between being a manager and being a leader. He was the first one to communicate this difference, even if it is a concept that seems obvious to us now. This article was awarded first prize for being the best *Harvard Business Review* article of the year and it stimulated a whole new line of research. His contentious article suggested that, not only are leaders and managers different kinds of people, but they do different things:

- *Leaders.* Have entirely personal attitudes towards their goals; their goals appear to be embedded in themselves. They put energy into projecting goals as visions that excite others and work with them to turn the image into reality. Leaders tend to be more solitary and introverted, and relate not to job titles but to individuals in an intuitive and empathic way. Leaders tend to identify with the broad picture.
- *Managers.* Regard goals as entirely impersonal and reactive and tend not to develop goals for themselves. They see their job as organising the resources and the people to ensure that goals are achieved. Managers prefer to work with people and relate to people according to their job descriptions or organisational status. They belong to their environment and depend on relationships and roles for their identity.

Zaleznik believed that there was an inherent conflict between the development of both leaders and managers in an organisation. Each hold different attitudes towards their goals, careers, relations with others and their self-perception. As they are different kinds of people, Zaleznik conjectured that conditions favouring the growth of one might be detrimental to the other.

He claimed in the article that our current educational process and the bureaucratic nature of most organisations breed managers. On that basis, he seems to feel that leaders are an endangered species. If organisations wish to develop leaders, they need to foster mentors and close, one-to-one relationships between senior and junior staff. Developing leaders entails a culture of individualism and possibly elitism which runs counter to the conservative, group-based culture of large organisations.

In short, managers enjoy relating with people, they attain much of their sense of self from such activities and they work to maintain order. Leaders, on the other hand, are loners, risk takers and visionaries.

TRANSFORMATION AND TRANSACTION

In 1978, James MacGregor-Burns published a book entitled simply *Leadership* in which he agreed that there were significant differences between managers and leaders. Unlike Zaleznik, Burns argued that both were necessary. He called them transformational leaders and transactional managers, terminology that is familiar from the Burke–Litwin model.

- Transformational leaders do things that change the organisation.
- Transactional managers keep the organisation going in the same direction.

Burns pointed out that every organisation needs both elements in all of its managers. There are shades of situational leadership here as the shifting emphasis between transactional and transformational styles is driven by the needs of the internal and external environment. However, this combination of skills may be difficult for some people to achieve. These, in tabular form, are the characteristics that MacGregor-Burns believes distinguished transactional managers and transformational leaders:

	Leaders	Managers
Emotional involvement	Emotionally involved with ideals and vision	Involved with tasks and people associated with the tasks
Personal life	Work and private life are indistinguishable and merge with each other	Attempt to maintain boundaries seeing a proper time for each
Achieving commitment and accountability	Inspire. Hold people accountable by inducing feelings of guilt	Involve people. Use contracts, performance appraisal and key result areas
Value emphasis	Concerned with what they are trying to build	How to build their contractual piece
Problems	Create problems	Solve them
Planning	Long-range	Short to medium term
Responses	Appreciate contrariness and people who argue	Like people who conform
Relations	Engender feelings of love and hate. Create non-stable relationships	Tend to have more predictable relationships and do not create strong feelings

Summary

Burns' profile of the transformational leader is that of a visionary, solitary, inspirational person; a charismatic character with a great deal of empathy who seeks to involve followers in the mission. They are able to assess not only the mission, but also the goals which correspond to the needs of their followers. Their primary goal is change and they are probably less concerned with how to achieve the result than with the mission itself.

Transactional managers, on the other hand, prefer teamwork, task accomplishment and problem solving. They have a steadier way of working with others and they view the leader–follower relationship as a process of exchange.

However, Burns admits that, though they are different, transactional managers and transformational leaders need each other, they complement and supplement each other:

> For clarity of goals and direction, managers need leaders. For indispensable help in reaching their goals, leaders need managers.

Conclusion

The work of Zaleznik and McGregor–Burns has highlighted an essential difference between managers and leaders. Zaleznik points out that the two differ in their treatment of goals with leaders tending to develop a vision and using other people to achieve it. Managers tend to be the people who set about achieving the goals, rather than setting them, a view supported by Burns who distinguished between transformational leaders who bring about change and transactional managers who keep the organisation going in the direction that has been set by the leader. Their work marked a watershed in leadership studies.

LEADING BY EMPOWERMENT

Introduction

With the work of Zaleznik and Burns, the history of leadership seems to have passed through a watershed, but we should not assume that the past has been forgotten. In this section we look at work which brings leadership studies right up to date.

Bennis and Nanus: Taking Charge

In 1985, Warren Bennis and Burt Nanus published a book called *Leaders – the Strategies for Taking Charge*. What is significant about this book is that it seems to have moved full circle back to great man theory; however, their research results were very different.

They identified 90 top people who, by common consensus, were regarded as leaders in different fields, including business, spiritual communities, the arts, hospitals and sport. Irrespective of their environment, these leaders were deemed to exemplify contemporary leadership. The biggest difference from great man theory was that these leaders were alive; the researchers could talk to them and the people who worked with them.

The research carried out by Bennis and Nanus was comprehensive, yet their conclusions are extremely simple and focus on four major areas:

- The management of attention
- The management of meaning
- The management of trust
- The management of self.

The Management of Attention

Put another way, managers need to create vision, catch people's attention, draw their eye and keep it focused on the goal. Most important is the ability to paint a tangible picture of what that vision is:

> On the one hand, an organisation seeks to maximise its rewards from its position in the external environment; and on the other hand individuals seek to maximise their reward from participation in the organisation. When the organisation has a clear sense of purpose, direction and desired future, and when this image is widely shared, individuals are able to find their own roles, both in the organisation and in the larger society of which they are a part. This empowers

individuals and confers status upon them because they see themselves as part of a worthwhile enterprise.

The leader with a compelling vision can draw other people in, and that vision is essential to build confidence in people, inspire them and turn purpose into action.

The researchers recognise the problems of being a worker in an organisation that does not confer status on the individual because it does not see itself as a worthwhile enterprise. They believe that it is far better for staff to feel proud of being part of an organisation's activities:

> They gain a sense of importance as they are transformed from robots blindly following instructions into human beings engaged in a creative, purposeful venture. When individuals feel they can make a difference and that they can improve the society in which they are living through their participation in an organisation, it is much more likely that they will bring vigour and enthusiasm to their tasks and that the results of their work will be mutually reinforcing. Under these conditions, the human energies of the organisations are aligned towards a common end and a major precondition for success has been satisfied.

In simple terms, the researchers tell us we need to get people excited about their contribution to the success of the organisation. The good leader knows exactly what he wants from people and gives them confidence. This is not a new idea, but it is one of the essential ingredients of leadership. The leader's attitude must be:

> We have seen what this organisation can be, we understand the consequences of that vision, and now we must act to make it so.

A vision cannot be established by edict or the exercise of power or coercion, it is an act of persuasion. Leaders must create an enthusiastic and dedicated commitment to that vision. Once that commitment is there, a unity is created between leaders and followers.

The Management of Meaning

It is not enough to have a vision if it cannot be communicated. People have to be aligned behind the idea, they must all be working in the same direction and that only comes about through effective communication. There are a number of key requirements:

- Organisations depend on shared meanings. Leaders can articulate things that may have been unspoken and they focus people on key issues.
- The style of communication is important in effectively managing how meaning is shared and used to drive an organisation.
- The meaning must be framed in such a way that people pay attention to it at every level.

How do leaders get people aligned behind the organisation's goals? How do they communicate visions? The authors answered this question partially by asserting that this can happen through 'the management of meaning'. But this doesn't go far enough because it fails to indicate how this actually happens, how the leader creates the understanding, participation and ownership of the vision.

Bennis and Nanus call the process by which employees align themselves to a vision 'the social architecture'.

> We believe that we human beings are suspended in webs of significance that we ourselves have spun. We view social architecture to be those webs of meaning . . . Social architecture is that which provides context or meaning and commitment to its members and stakeholders. First and foremost, social architecture presents a shared interpretation of organisational events, so that members know how they are expected to behave. It also generates a commitment to the primary organisational values and philosophy – that is, the vision that employees feel they are working for and can believe in. Finally, an organisation's social architecture serves as a control mechanism, sanctioning or proscribing particular kinds of behaviour.

To transform the social architecture, three things have to be done:

- Create a new and compelling vision capable of bringing the workforce to a new place, this process is described in the section on the management of attention.
- Develop commitment for the new vision. The organisation must be mobilised to accept and support the new vision to make it happen. Commitment requires more than verbal compliance, more than just dialogue and exchange. The vision has to be

articulated clearly and frequently in a variety of ways. This would include statements of policy that have minimum impact, revising recruiting aims and methods, training that is explicitly geared to modify behaviour in support of new organisational values and, not the least, adapting and modifying shared symbols that signal and reinforce the new vision.

- Institutionalise the new vision. The authors quote a story about a Chinese general, Sun Tzu, who lived two and a half thousand years ago. The king ordered Sun Tzu to train his army, and the general, after drilling and disciplining them to his satisfaction, asked the king to inspect his troops. The king replied that he didn't want to but the general replied, 'the king is only fond of words and cannot translate them into deeds'.

Words, symbols, articulation, training and recruiting, while necessary, don't go far enough. Changes in the management processes, the organisational structure, and management style must all support the changes in the pattern of values and behaviour that a new vision implies. Translating intention into reality involves not only organisational mission, structure and human resources, but also the political and cultural forces that drive the system. The leadership must be willing to 'walk the talk' even when this might be uncomfortable and distasteful.

Leaders have to involve people in building their own new world as part of the vision they have provided. Aristotle said:

> The soul . . . never thinks without a picture.

The Management of Trust

Trust is hard to describe. Indeed, trust is an historical concept. We require repeated interaction with another person before we recognise that it might exist! Observers trust people who are predictable and who make their positions known. Leaders must continually strive to earn trust and maintain it. By clearly stating the vision and sticking to it, the organisation earns trust. Visual identity and clear, consistent corporate statements are two of the more visible forms of integrity; organisations that work hard to defend their identity and demonstrate staying power earn trust.

> Trust is the emotional glue that binds followers and leaders together. The accumulation of trust is a measure of the legitimacy of leadership. It cannot be mandated or purchased. It must be earned. Trust is the basic ingredient of all organisations, the basic lubricant that maintains communities. It is as mysterious and illusive a concept as leadership and it is as important.

In organisations, trust between leaders and followers cannot exist without two conditions:

- The leader's vision for the organisation must be clear, attractive and attainable. We tend to trust leaders who create these visions, since vision represents the context for shared beliefs in a common organisational purpose.
- The leader's position must be clear. We tend to trust leaders when we know where they stand in relation to the organisation and how they position the organisation relative to the environment.

Positioning and trust are fundamental to all leadership activities.

- All leaders face the challenge of overcoming resistance to change. Some try to do this by the simple exercise of power and control, but effective leaders learn that there are better ways to overcome resistance to change. This involves the achievement of voluntary commitment to shared values.
- A leader must reconcile the needs of different groups inside and outside the organisation. He or she must be sensitive to their various needs and have a clear sense of the organisation's position.
- The leader is responsible for the set of ethics or norms that govern the behaviour of people in the organisation. Leaders can establish a set of ethics by demonstrating their commitment to the set of ethics they are trying to institutionalise.

Trust, integrity and positioning are all different faces of a common property of leadership – the ability to integrate those who must act with that which must be done so that it all comes together as a single organism in harmony with itself and its niche in the environment.

The Management of Self

Bennis and Nanus believe that managers and leaders must develop their own skills so that they form an important resource within the organisation. There is too much emphasis on formal tasks and not enough on 'human aspects'. Executives may spend up to 90% of their time with subordinates, so they need to become competent in interpersonal skills such as listening, dealing with conflict, and nurturing and developing others so that they can manage themselves and others. The first step for leaders, they believe, is to focus on their own fallibility as an opportunity to learn and improve.

Leading is an entirely personal business and people must learn to continue working at their talents . . . and their weaknesses. Leaders need not have all the skills themselves; they build teams to compensate. The interviews that Bennis and Nanus conducted showed that leaders have discovered not just how to learn, but how to learn in an organisational context. They are able to concentrate on what matters most to the organisation and to use the organisation as a learning environment. Successful leaders have developed a set of skills that have become known as the 'new competence':

- Acknowledging and sharing uncertainty.
- Embracing error.
- Responding to the future.
- Becoming interpersonally competent.
- Gaining self-knowledge.

Bennis and Nanus found many examples of how leaders acknowledge and share uncertainty in task-force settings with colleagues. They used their mistakes as learning experiences and engaged in goal-setting exercises to force re-examination of current assumptions and priorities. They used their interpersonal skills to encourage others to join in the search for new ideas, and they constantly enhanced their understanding of their own limits and biases by testing their views against those of knowledgeable colleagues and outside experts.

Leading by Empowerment

Bennis and Nanus also talked to the people who worked for the leaders they had identified and studied. When they asked them what it was like to work with them, the subordinates replied that they felt empowered. That feeling had four principal components:

- They felt that they made a difference, they were not just a payroll number. Coming to work made them feel good because they knew they were needed.
- Every day was a new learning experience.
- They felt that they belonged to an important community and they were united by a common purpose.
- Above all, they felt that they had fun at work with those leaders.

Leadership Myths

Bennis and Nanus concluded their review of leadership by looking at some common myths:

- Leadership is a rare skill. The authors anticipate the later view of multiple leadership by pointing out that, although great leaders are rare, there are vast numbers of leaders throughout society.
- Leaders are born not made. Making a further attack on great man theory and trait theory, the authors asserted that leaders can be made through training and experience.
- Leaders are charismatic. The authors believed that charisma results from effective leadership, it is not a condition of it.
- Leadership exists only at the top of an organisation. By focusing on top leaders, researchers may be overlooking the very large number of routine leadership roles that exist in large organisations.
- The leader controls, directs, prods, manipulates. Leadership is about the empowerment of others, and leaders are able to translate intentions into reality by aligning the energies of others.

Conclusion

Bennis and Nanus, in their study of 90 contemporary leaders, have shown that leaders face new challenges in overcoming a lack of commitment, poor management credibility and an increasingly complex leadership environment. They can overcome these problems and achieve successful leadership by creating a compelling vision, communicating it effectively, building trust in their vision and their leadership and constantly developing their own interpersonal and oral skills. By using those skills effectively, leaders can empower other people to achieve their vision and ensure organisational success.

They summarised the difference between managing and leading:

> Managers are people who do things right
> Leaders are people who do the right thing.

THE 1992 VIEW . . . WHAT LEADERS REALLY DO

John P. Kotter, Professor of Organizational Behavior at Harvard Business School and author of a number of books on leadership, continued the managers versus leaders debate started by Zaleznik some 15 years earlier. His work confirmed the general trend in the debate over leadership requirements. In a 1992 article entitled 'What leaders really do?' he signalled agreement with Zaleznik:

> Leaders are different from managers, but not for the reasons that people think.

However, he dismissed the arguments about leadership being dependent on charisma or exotic personality traits, and stated that leadership was certainly not for the chosen few. Kotter argued that organisations needed both managers and leaders in the plural.

> With careful selection, nurturing and encouragement, dozens of people can play important leadership roles.

Kotter's view is that the real challenge facing organisations is to combine strong management and strong leadership and use them to balance each other. The essential difference he believes is that:

> Good management controls complexity; effective leadership produces useful change.

What organisations need to do is recognise the differences, get the right people into the right roles and work hard to make them part of the same team. Kotter identified a number of differences between management and leadership – some of them familiar from earlier findings. His views also reflected Bennis and Nanus' conclusion that leaders and managers have to operate in an increasingly complex environment.

- Managers manage complexity by planning and budgeting. They set specific goals and allocate resources to achieve them.
- Leaders deal with the complexity by setting a direction for constructive change. They provide a vision and lay down the changes needed to achieve it.
- Managers achieve their plans by organising and staffing. They create an organisational structure, then implement and monitor to ensure compliance.
- Leaders align people to a vision so that they are committed and contribute to it.

Creating Leadership Values

Despite Kotter's beliefs, he felt that organisations are not achieving that balance between strong leadership and strong management. Even if organisations are good at identifying people with leadership potential, they still need to develop them. Here, he reflects the earlier work by McCall and Lombardo who showed what makes a good leader. Kotter's ideal leaders would progress through stages:

- Significant challenge early in a career so that people learn something about the difficulties of leadership.
- Opportunity to undertake broad assignments later in a career through lateral career moves or involvement in broadly based task forces.

- Membership of informal networks which support multiple leadership opportunities.

Conclusion

Kotter has further emphasised the view that managers and leaders are different. However, he believed that they are complementary and that both are essential to organisational effectiveness. He made an important contribution to leadership theory by showing that organisations may need more than one leader – they can succeed by developing a network of multiple leaders, provided they are all working in the same direction.

SIX DEMANDS OF LEADERSHIP

With the publication of *Developing Leadership: A Look Ahead*, Morgan McCall (1993) provided a valuable critique of recent leadership thinking. He suggested that there are six key requirements for effective leadership:

1. *Setting direction.* Setting direction is dreaming what might be, gauging its feasibility, and figuring out what has to be done to pull it off. It requires using knowledge of the business and its technologies to create a vision for the future. It also requires the ability to design:
   - Organisational structure (to be consistent with the chosen direction may require something other than a traditional hierarchy).
   - Reward systems (structuring pay and other rewards to reinforce behaviour consistent with the direction).
   - Information flows (getting information and authority to the people in the best position to make decisions).
   - Staffing (identifying the kinds of skills people need to function effectively in the organisation).
2. *Alignment.* Success in achieving the chosen direction depends on effectively aligning key relationships. Critical relationships

include anyone whose co-operation is essential to success or whose opposition would represent a serious obstacle. New organisational forms that are built on coalitions and partnerships, doing business in an international marketplace, and the increasing diversity within the US labour market make it clear that leaders in this decade cannot get by with minimal alignment skills.

3. *Values.* The long-term ability of a leader to influence others hinges on credibility, integrity and trust. While short-term compliance can be extracted by threat, fear, and coercion, effective leaders are people who do what they say they will do when they say they will do it, and who let you know when, for some reason, they can't. They treat other people with dignity and respect, even if those other people are different from themselves.

4. *Temperament.* A person who is thrown by ambiguity, folds up in the face of criticism, goes down with setbacks, or loses confidence in tight spots will have a tough time as a leader in the stress and change of the next ten years. Certain qualities make up a temperament for leadership – a manner of thinking, behaving and reacting that helps an individual operate with relative comfort in a job characterised by making decisions under uncertainty, being at the mercy of uncontrollable and capricious forces, and being responsible for large numbers of people, pounds and resources.

5. *Self-awareness.* Self-awareness, a realistic assessment of one's own strength and weaknesses, is a prerequisite for understanding other people's perspectives, empowering others, taking risks and absorbing failures. For leaders, self-awareness is crucial to knowing their own limits, knowing what they really want to do and what they are willing to sacrifice to get it, taking responsibility for their own careers and growth, and being ready to seize opportunities when they appear.

6. *Growth.* Because leadership is complex, and because the demands on leaders are constantly changing, leaders themselves must constantly learn, grow and change. Situations are moving targets, and the leaders who fit a specific situation today will be misfits tomorrow unless they can adapt and change as rapidly as their context. Continual growth is no longer a luxury for leaders, it is a fundamental requirement.

The Language of Leadership

Many of the leadership studies have focused on the importance of oral communication to the work of leaders and managers. Leaders manage by inspiration; they must be able to craft an organisation's mission and vision and they must have the skills to communicate that vision in a way that inspires others to act.

Jay Conger of McGill University, in an article 'Inspiring others; the language of leadership' (1991), argued that few managers possess the necessary communications skills to empower others, and he felt that the business culture and education system may even discourage them. Business language cannot convey the range of energy and emotion a leader needs to succeed. Like politicians, leaders must learn to sell themselves and their messages.

To do this they must learn two skills:

- Framing.
- Rhetorical crafting.

Framing

Framing is the process of defining the purpose of the organisation in a meaningful way. Effective framing of an organisational mission will ensure emotional impact, particularly in terms of building a sense of confidence and excitement about the future.

For example, one group of staff was told that a project had an 80% chance of success, while the other group was told that there was a 20% risk of failure. Naturally, more staff supported the first project, giving it a much higher chance of success.

Rhetorical Techniques

Conger's studies showed that, apart from appealing to emotions or shared ideals, inspiring leaders use a number of techniques such as metaphor, different language styles, rhythmic devices or para-language to ensure impact. These techniques have proved to be effective and they can be easily learned. Conger summarised the key skills needed to share vision:

- Use more analogies, metaphors and stories when speaking.
- Keep the message simple and focused, and repeat it consistently.
- Experiment with various rhetorical techniques.
- Allow your own emotions to surface as you speak. If you are excited or concerned, show it.
- Do not pretend to be an expert in areas where the audience know that you are not.
- Language skills can be misused and we must guard against the violation of the ethics of communication.

Conclusion

Effective oral communication is essential to effective leadership. By developing communication skills, Conger believes managers will be able to share their vision. Conger felt that, while organisations have learned a great deal about the necessity of strategic vision and effective leadership, they have overlooked vital links between the vision and the leader's ability to communicate it powerfully. Conger believed that leaders will not only have to be great strategists, but also communicators who can motivate an audience. When strategic goals are well understood, they are convincing and they ensure that subordinates will follow.

A FINAL VIEW OF THE WORK OF THE LEADER

At the beginning of this chapter, we mentioned Lieutenant General William P. Pagonis who led the 40 000 people who ran the theatre logistics during the Gulf War. Pagonis' thoughts on the success of leadership during the Gulf War reflect many of the themes described earlier in this book. Pagonis came to a number of broad conclusions:

- Leadership is only possible where the ground has been prepared in advance. In his case, he explained how the army went to great lengths to grow and develop its leaders.

- That preparation only worked if the leader demonstrated two traits, expertise and empathy.
- Leaders take active roles in remaking the environment so that it supports the exercise and culture of leadership.

Overall, he believed that leadership is a function of personal and organisational qualities:

- Charisma or personal presence was an essential quality in situations of war, but the leader had to earn the trust of the troops long before any crisis.
- A leader had to demonstrate expertise in any area where he held responsibility. That expertise was useless without empathy.

On the question of organisational development, Pagonis explained that leaders could not function without a leadership-supporting environment.

- Effective delegation ensures that leaders can fill gaps in their own expertise.
- System building ensures that information from these centres of expertise flows back to the leader.
- Delegation and information flow work effectively when everyone shared the vision or organisational goal. Pagonis used short, simple phrases such as 'good logistics is combat power'.
- Educating subordinates ensures that everyone understands the vision and the group's shared objectives.
- Formal communications and feedback help to complement the chain of command and ensure that a leader aggressively pursues contact with colleagues and subordinates.

Pagonis' observations do not constitute any rigorous attempt at defining leadership, but they do provide a useful insight into a practising leader who has adopted many of the findings we have reviewed in this book and used them to run a successful operation in a complex environment.

> Leaders must be motivators, educators, role models, sounding boards, confessors and cheerleaders . . . Successful leadership is not mysterious. Leaders must set their own agendas and use the tools and techniques best suited to help them achieve their goals.

A Final Thought

The challenge that we face in this leadership debate is to understand that, at the very least, Anatole France was close to the mark when he wrote

> To accomplish great things, we must not only act but dream, not only plan but also believe.

Chapter Five
VISION . . . IS HAVING THE IMAGE OF THE CATHEDRAL AS WE CARVE THE GRANITE

Leadership is more than brave words and the encouragement of others to do courageous deeds. Central to our current understanding of leadership is the capacity and willingness of leadership to create 'a vision of what could be'. Vision is about having the picture of the cathedral as we carve the granite (or perhaps plane the pews or even lay the pipes for the central heating).

'Any company that cannot imagine the future won't be around to enjoy it' wrote Hamel and Prahalad in 1994. Kotter (1996) was as forceful when he wrote 'without an appropriate vision, a transformation effort can easily dissolve into a list of confusing, incompatible and time-consuming projects that go in the wrong direction or nowhere at all.'

In our model, we recognise the centrality of visioning, as a pivotal activity of leadership. The essential thrust of all the serious thinking from Burns, through Bennis and Nanus to Kotter makes that centrality inevitable.

The central part played by 'the vision of what could be' in an organisation's drive to improvement is further enhanced by three additional themes.

- By communication. It has been estimated that a failure to communicate the vision, by a factor of 10 (or 100 or even 1000) is one of the prime causes of the failure of many transformation activities (Kotter, 1996). It seems to us to be axiomatic that a vision that is known, understood and acted upon only by a small proportion of those who might be affected by it, is destined to be worse than useless.

- By the building of trust. Without the development of trust, in the leadership, in the vision and in each other, we have eliminated an essential pre-condition of transformation success.
- By the building of an aligned culture. A vision which fails to address the need to bring about an alignment of the culture of the future, with the organisation's sense of its own destiny, may never reach the starting blocks of transformation.

Many people find themselves uncomfortable with words like 'vision'; was it a British prime minister who asked sneeringly 'what is this vision thing?'. There is often a marked distaste to trade in language like this. It appears to be outside the usual range of 'hardnosed' and comfortable business words such as targets, goals, results, below the line, strategic imperatives and so on. Visioning, then, appears to some people to border on effete nonsense, fanciful impracticality or simple 'airy-fairy' thinking. This is an issue that needs to be confronted and dispelled at once by anyone trying to bring about change.

Without a clear and compelling vision:

- Plans can be turned into budgets to relate logically to timetables and then strategies but, once this has all been done, nobody will know what it was all intended to achieve or even why success mattered in the first place.
- Only one person (or perhaps a very small group) will know what new directions need to be followed and they will need to spend most of their time in planning and directing the work of subordinates so that things move in the required direction.
- Employees will only be able to face new circumstances by referring back to rule books, manuals and 'custom and practice'.
- Turning up for work will be all that matters. Indeed, trying to be part of anything new, different or creative is likely to be seen as painful and counter-productive.

We know, from experience, that having to direct the work of thousands of people in detail is time consuming and wasteful and that it is much easier if work can be done by groups of people who know where they are headed and who can solve problems for themselves as they go along. We have all been fired by enthusiasm in our own lives by the words and ideas of a few teachers, politicians, friends with absorbing interests, authors and playwrights who have picked us up and showed us how things could be different. Why then should we feel embarrassed and awkward about extending this to our work, our colleagues and the people who work for us? If the language of visioning seems a little uncomfortable then we must address the potential reasons for such unease within ourselves rather than blame it on the words themselves. Any tug-of-war team knows perfectly well about the need for everyone to pull in the same direction and why they are doing it. 'Woolly' words that make us feel embarrassed about how we communicate a shared purpose and enthusiasm usually imply a lack of vision rather than an absence of clarity or sense of purpose.

This chapter will start by reviewing the work that highlights the importance of managers having a clear vision. It will continue with some more practical perspectives on how a sense of vision can be developed and communicated and conclude by looking at the mission statements that are often used to guide and reflect the generality of a vision into the day-by-day workings of an organisation.

WHY VISION IS IMPORTANT

Organisational research, as we have seen, shows that managerial skills are best understood as forming two complementary clusters: one set relates to goal setting, problem analysis, and effective decision-making; the other to providing a framework about organisational purpose and the employee's role in accomplishing it. While the former is important for getting specific jobs done, the latter shapes the character of an underlying set of attitudes shared by a team of workers. Creating these more fundamental attitudes can make all the difference; they can cause enthusiasm and commitment on the one hand, or lassitude and a devil-may-care climate on the other. Vision, when well communicated, can make even dull jobs rewarding.

Very little has been written concerning the role which vision claims in the strategic capability of organisations to flex with changing pressures and demands of the global market. Recently the best known strategic work has been done by Christopher A. Bartlett and Sumantra Ghoshal (1994) in three papers for *Harvard Business Review*. The first of these – 'Changing the role of top management: Beyond strategy to purpose' – reinforces an essential shift from management doctrines based on strategy, structure and systems to a broader perspective created by considerations of purpose, process and people.

The mindset of successful practising managers which derived from the concept that the leader designs strategy, builds the structures and manages the systems which drive the company forward, held good through a half- century which saw the creation and development of world leading organisations. The systems which provided the discipline, focus and control after the upheaval of World War Two, depended on the reduction of the effects of human idiosyncrasies by designing tightly knit planning and control structures.

This approach, undoubtedly effective over many years, no longer suffices to cope with the runaway technological, competitive and market changes of the last decade. Today technologies and markets fuse together, spawning whole new industries which may overtake or replace the traditional industries which gave them birth. Witness the fact that more than 30% of 3M's sales derive from products introduced during the last five years, or that Canon have expanded from cameras to computers by exploiting the opportunities of the calculator and copier markets.

The muscularity demonstrated by large corporations which have continued to flourish rests with their move to a more organic approach, which recognises dependency on that rarest of corporate reserves: the knowledge and expertise of front-line staff. By paying attention to 'soft issues' and by involving staff in determining the businesses purpose, these large corporations have flourished. The management processes which have enabled this to happen have less emphasis on controlling mechanisms and a lot more emphasis on development.

The companies which have moved ahead have recognised the

need for strategy to be created from the front line where the managers really know what is going on. The old assumption that the CEO has full strategic responsibility ignores the fact that knowledge and expertise change too fast for news to travel up the old management structures. Andy Grove of Intel recognised that the move from memory chips to microprocessors was really effected by the activities of hands-on project leaders, market managers and plant supervisors who were literally 'formulating strategy with their finger tips'.

It is increasingly clear that crafting overall corporate strategic frameworks and applying the framework by logic is self-defeating in today's real world. Quantitative planning and control processes do not reward and motivate the front line finger-tip strategists whose corporate loyalty is constantly eroded by restructuring, re-trenching and the role ambiguity often created. There is increased devolvement of strategy to 'business units' with the concomitant demand to fit 'their' strategies into the corporate rationale. The writers suggest that the resultant disaffection and cynicism is only overcome by creating an essential emotional link to the organisation.

One prescription for this link, the totally focused intent to challenge and overcome specific rivals by defining targets in competitive terms only, has proved in the long term to be constraining and has not liberated the rapid response creativity on which survival and growth depend.

Komatsu, which targeted Caterpillar obsessively at the end of the last decade, found that this single-minded approach fostered stereotyped thinking and stagnation. President Tatsuya Ketada coined a new slogan: 'Growth, Global, Groupwide' (3 Gs) to reflect a more abstract and liberating challenge for middle- and front-line managers who needed to go out and explore the opportunities for operating in a creative and innovative way 'always encouraging initiative from below'. The abstract nature of the 3Gs slogan stimulated people to ask what they could do and to respond creatively.

However, strategic visions which are too broad to convey meaning and guidance through the organisational layers can be meaningless. The purpose is to embed a well-articulated corporate ambition which still gives freedom to the individual to interpret the company's broad objectives in a relevant and practical context. The writers propose three criteria which differentiate this approach from previous practice:

- The vision is expressed in terms which capture the attention of employees. Kotter (1996) suggests that if you cannot describe the vision in five minutes or less and get a reaction that signifies both understanding and interest, you have failed.
- The organisation is engaged in developing, defining and renewing the ambition.
- It is translated into measurable activities to provide a benchmark for achievement and maintain momentum.

An example is Bob Allen of AT&T's effort to express an ambition neither too rational or analytical, too focused on threatening competition, nor too technologically futuristic, by choosing a very human register dedicating the company to 'become the world's best at bringing people together, giving them easy access to each other and to the information and services they want and need, anytime, anywhere' – simple direct language understood on a very personal level.

A good vision statement invites and requires the total involvement of the organisation in carrying the ambition forward into operation through a process of interpretation and refining. At AT&T the whole organisation was challenged to interpret and make operational the 'anytime, anywhere' statement. Allen created a strategy forum and invited the 60 most senior managers to define the overall objectives and direction required – a significant commitment of time and expertise.

At Komatsu a 'committee for the 1990s' was set up to determine how to enrich corporate philosophy, broaden social contributions and revitalise human resources.

Once objectives are more defined, given a practical interpretation, the organisation needs to commit even more strongly in order to build and sustain belief. At Corning where the focus was on core capabilities overlaid with a commitment to world class quality, the CEO allocated $5 million to create a Quality Institute, leading a massive education and development programme, boosting training to 5% of every employee's working hours. Renewed self respect and self-confidence in Corning's people paid off.

AT&T followed through by investing in complementary information technologies, vital to new communication highways, at a cost in excess of $20 million to demonstrate the vision's legitimacy and boost belief in its viability.

The emotional attachment is strongest when the employee can understand and identify with what the company stands for. If employees are expected to make extraordinary efforts to realise company targets they must be able to commit to them. Companies that boldly assert what they stand for typically attract and retain committed workers who are satisfied with a set of values. The 'quirky' ethics and philosophy of Anita Roddick's Body Shop appeals not only to customers, but grabs the imagination and enthusiasm of young people working for the organisation.

Three lessons emerge for top management:

- Build on the existing values and beliefs.
- Maintain over time a high level of personal involvement in the activity.
- Translate broad philosophical objectives into visible and measurable goals.

New values cannot be imposed. A resistant cynicism for the 'culture of the month' is likely to be the result. Building on strengths, modifying existing values, confronting with care, are required.

New values need more than speeches. Daily actions are what carry the message. Corning's CEO talked and listened to his workers on a regular programme of visits, reiterating new values and taking steps to reinforce broad idealistic values – for example, 'breaking the glass ceiling' for women, minorities and non-US nationals.

Progress needs to be measured. At Corning the commitment to becoming a 'world-class company' was embodied in the objective of becoming publicly recognised by inclusion in the annual *Fortune* CEO poll of 'America's most admired corporations' – based not only on financial results, but performance on quality, innovation and corporate responsibility.

The organisations which hold on to really committed people are those which understand that more than providing just work, they can help give meaning to people's lives. These organisations treat the employees as an asset to be developed, not simply a cost to be controlled. As a result they 'belong' to the organisation. They are not mercenaries but marines! The companies which are forging this new kind of bond are those that:

- Recognise individual accomplishments.
- Give personal recognition to contributions.
- Commit to developing employees.
- Foster individual initiative.

Newsletters, social functions, relaxation of dress codes, all can help humanise corporate life, but they are but devices and cannot replace the face-to-face recognition from senior managers at a personal level, at work. Empty public relations gestures are seen as manipulative, employees want to see genuine support in troubled times for the business.

In the mid 1980s Intel's Andy Groves made strenuous efforts to avoid lay-offs in the face of a $200 million loss, by first selling a 20% interest in the business to IBM, then asking for 10 hours a week more from everyone, then a 10% wage cut. These actions asked a lot from people, but also expressed genuine concern for the livelihoods of individual employees. As such they were likely to stimulate a co-operative reciprocal response and foster loyalty.

Development needs to go beyond training for job skills if it is to be viewed as a commitment to personal growth. Body Shop established an education centre going much further than training in company products or customer care, adding sessions on sociology, AIDS, ageing, etc., while the CEO of a Danish-based commercial cleaning business (ISS), has gone beyond basic job skills and uses training as a 'demonstration of caring'. A five-stage programme for cleaning-team supervisors covers topics such as financial knowledge, interpersonal skills, problem solving and customer relations, transforming 'work gang bosses' into effective team builders and new business generators.

Individual initiative was harnessed at 3M by confirming belief in the entrepreneurs within the organisation. A 15% rule encourages employees to use up to that percentage of work time to investigate products they personally believe have potential for the company. Many 'bootleg' innovations developed into important businesses for 3M and the legends of home-grown heroes have served to motivate further effort by keeping alive the belief that individual effort is prized.

Finally, Bartlett and Ghoshal (1994) summarise the crucial importance of purpose in separating those organisations which continue to be defined and confined as profit-making entities from those whose broader purpose can embrace a pivotal social role which in turn can enrol their human resources in the attainment of success. At a time when other social institutions are weakening, the corporation potentially occupies an important place, beyond being a business, as:

- a repository of state-of-the-art resources and knowledge.
- a wealth generator.
- an agent of social change.
- a forum of social interaction and personal fulfilment.

Purpose is the statement of a company's moral response to its broadly defined responsibilities, not an amoral plan for exploiting commercial opportunity. Self-serving organisational values coupled with the narrow focus of self-interest, lose the excitement, support, commitment and pride typical of successful organisations which recognise that purpose, rather than strategy, is the key, and that the definition and expression of that purpose is a prime requirement of today's leaders.

WHAT VISION IS

A vision is the way we may link everyday events to a large set of values. Managers who communicate a vision are able to say why their company is important in the larger scheme of things. They comfortably link small jobs to larger frame issues; they have a sense of purpose and seem to make life at work more meaningful.

Managers with vision are able to step back from a problem and see it in a much larger context. They do not let the frustration of each immediate issue cloud their understanding of more general directions.

Managerial vision can be communicated in clear, elementary images. For example, all the great religious teachers of the past have used story telling to teach. Jesus, Mohammed, and the Buddha all used short tales to convey basic precepts about life's meaning, ideas that have been remembered for centuries in story form. But it is not only religious leaders who used well-chosen stories and images to communicate. For example, military leaders are great proponents of using stories to create visions for their men. Listen carefully to the most successful political speechmakers. Moving speeches have a straightforward style. They draw on simple events and experiences, on a set of shared symbols, and they try to tie specific activities and events into life's broader meanings.

In the modern world most managers have drawn away from story-telling, mottos, and from symbolic speech. Our schools generally tell us that poetic skills are imprecise, old fashioned, and unbusinesslike. We are taught that the more mathematically we can state a problem, the more scientific is our thinking. We are also taught to use abstract words and jargon instead of ordinary language. We are encouraged to talk about 'human resources' instead of people and about 'organisational behaviour' instead of about what people do at work. Oddly enough, those who still do have old-fashioned communication skills often become the most successful managers. People like to work with associates who can tell a story, who can see the humour in a difficult moment, and who view life in this broader sense. In a word, these are the managers with vision.

HOW VISIONING FITS WITH OTHER MANAGEMENT SKILLS

Being a good story-teller, colourfully linking small things to larger values, is not a substitute for pragmatic managerial skills. With vision alone, one is little more than an entertaining dreamer or folk philosopher. Managers must, first and foremost, be able to identify both excellence and its opposite, and to see their implications in a full range of specific performance contexts. A manager must be able to set goals, to coach, to stay in control of his/her time and responsibilities, and to make tough decisions. But in a modern business setting, uncertainty and change are key problems.

Furthermore, peer and subordinate support are often weak, especially when it comes to carrying out the important tasks and priorities modern managers are assigned. Leadership and the ability to develop a vision are the extra skills needed to unite one's work team at these times of challenge. What will work without vision in good times requires vision as an added element when the going gets really tough. The skills of vision are more intuitive, less hard-nosed, and more informal tools than the problem-focused skills the manager must begin with. But vision is a necessary addition for continued success.

Creating the Vision

Here – broadly adapted from the ideas expressed by Peter Block in his seminal book *The Empowered Manager* (1987) and some of our own past colleagues who have worked on these – are some guidelines for developing and creating your own vision:

- Do not claim to be 'simply the best'. The wish to be 'better than all the rest', the winner, number one or anything else that smacks of simple recognition, fame or fortune has little place in a vision statement. Look instead for ways of showing the contribution that we can offer to all the stakeholders. If some of these stakeholders recognise our success and then chose to reward us – well and good; but this is not why we worked towards a vision. We pursued it because it was worth pursuing for its own sake.
- Don't be afraid of idealism. We expect most communications in a business world to reflect facts, numbers and data that are put forward with logic and rationality. We are often taught to be practical and pragmatic and to lead from the head rather than from the heart. Developing a vision requires us to venture into what for many will be less charted waters of idealism, spirituality and feeling. The key point here is that we need a vision to point us

to the organisation we really want even if we know or suspect that we will, actually, never get to that point. The direction is what we want. We need to stand on the ridge and see the mountain beckoning us in the distance. We most certainly do not want anyone at this stage wanting us to sketch out the route plan as to how we get there.

- Think first about your customers. The essential logic of this point is that your survival ultimately depends on whether your customers are prepared to keep doing business with you.

This may mean looking at departments or units as internal customers and this may in turn mean that we no longer see them as competitors for resources or influence. By looking at the influence of customers we can raise questions to extend the scope of a vision:

- If these internal or external customers were the only ones we could ever get, would we want to treat them any differently?
- Can we obtain feedback from them to help us improve what we do? Do we learn from dissatisfied customers or do we ignore them, act defensively and try to do our best to minimise any future interaction with them?
- If we find that we cannot fulfil our commitments how do we break the bad news? Do we acknowledge mistakes and try to improve, or do we look for scapegoats and ways of rationalising problems away as the fault of people or events beyond our control?
- How, in return, do we handle situations in which we ourselves are let down by our customers?

Translated into action terms these would give us vision statements along the lines of:

- We are committed to our customers' success.
- Our customers are as important to us as our shareholders.
- Our dissatisfied customers teach us how to sell to those who currently do not use our services or products.
- We are here to help, not to police.
- We don't force solutions on our customers.

These are just examples. Depending upon circumstances, these or statements like these might be generated to fit an organisation or department at a particular point of time.

- 'The customer cannot feel better about us than our employees feel about us.' These words from the CEO of Citibank may need pondering for a moment or two but the underlying message is particularly important. If we are to treat our external customers in the way they want then we cannot respond effectively to their needs if we are riven with internal disputes, misunderstandings, hostility and aggravation. When sales personnel meet customers they are likely to treat them in much the same way that they themselves are being treated. If we use punishment, threats to job security and autocratic management behaviour it is hardly surprising if employees pay us back by taking out the resentment they feel about us on those whom they are serving. How awful do the words 'Don't blame me, I only work here' continue to sound in customers' ears!

When we think about our own portion of the overall organisation we have a test-bed for what might be possible on the wider scale. When thinking about the vision for our own part of the business we can ask questions that might model more universally applicable issues. Some example questions could be:

- How do people celebrate success, support each other and get feedback to show that what they have done is correct and valued?
- How are conflict, disagreement and disharmony managed? Are these referred to others to settle or is there a climate in which useful arguments can be held?
- What is the appropriate balance between people doing things as a team and as skilled individuals who integrate the outcomes of their work with each other? Teamwork is often seen as the best way of doing things but may not always be the best way of using expensive resources.
- When does internal competition stop becoming motivating and start to become disruptive? (A trivial example perhaps, but we have actually seen a company 'It's a Knockout' sports day where

friendly rivalry degenerated into scuffles, appeals to the Chairman
to rule whether buckets had been properly filled, and hostility that
grew to the point where the event had to be abandoned.)

Many of these values can be incorporated into our vision of how the
people in the organisation should be viewed. As before, here are a
few examples from previous situations:

- We can disagree without fear.
- You have freedom to fail. You do not get shot for trying.
- Each person is connected with the final product.
- Every person is responsible for building the business.
- Everyone has a place at the table.

If Your Vision Statement Sounds a Little Embarrassing Then You Are Probably on the Right Track

A vision needs to express hope, a sense of unlimited possibility and
even idealism. The embarrassment we may feel is likely to be a
reflection of the radically different perspective we are having to
adopt from our usual business-like perspectives of caution, under-
statement, control and 'here and now' rationality. We feel, if not
naked then certainly unclothed, when forced to address issues that
speak to deeper values let alone those that may have a spiritual
component.

  According to Nanus (1992), powerful and transforming visions
tend to have the following special properties:

Appropriate

They are appropriate for the organisation and for the times. They fit
in terms of the organisation's history, culture and values, are
consistent with the organisation's present situation, and provide a
realistic and informed assessment of what is attainable in the future.
The organisation will almost certainly be changed, perhaps quite
radically. But if the vision is not appropriate for the organisation,
the time, cost and pain of transformation may be so great as to make

implementation of the vision all but impracticable. In this case a totally new organisation might be a better choice, as IBM found when it decided to enter the personal computer business.

Utopian

They set standards of excellence and reflect high ideals. They depict the organisation as a responsible community with a sense of integrity that strengthens and uplifts everyone in it.

Clarify Purpose

They clarify purpose and direction. They are persuasive and credible in defining what the organisation wants to make happen and, therefore, what are legitimate aspirations for people in the organisation. They provide agenda items that create focus and hold out hope and promise of a better tomorrow.

Inspire Enthusiasm

They inspire enthusiasm and encourage commitment. They widen the leader's support base by reflecting the needs and aspirations of many stakeholders, transcending differences in race, age, gender, and other demographic characteristics, and drawing stakeholders into a community of concerns about the future of the organisation.

Understandable

They are well articulated and easily understood. They are unambiguous enough to serve as a guide to strategy and action and to be internalised by those whose efforts are needed to turn the vision into reality.

Unique

They reflect the uniqueness of the organisation, its distinctive competence, what it stands for, and what it is able to achieve.

Ambitious

They are ambitious. They represent undisputed progress and expand the organisation's horizons. Often they call for sacrifice and emotional investment by followers, which are forthcoming because of the inherent attractiveness of the vision.

How to Communicate a Sense of Vision

In Chapter Four we outlined the work of Conger and his ideas on the language of leadership. He described the need for framing and rhetorical techniques. It is this need for honourable rhetoric that must drive the structure and communication of the vision. Extensive research in many varied fields has shown the enduring impact that comes from the use of simple images to enhance memorability. The images can be expressed in many ways – words, pictures or more abstract symbols. Here is a list of just some of the ways in which a vision can be portrayed, grouped into three categories:

WORDS	Text	The Koran; tales of the dervishes.
	Slogans	Liberty, equality, fraternity.
	Drama	Wagner's Ring Trilogy.
VISUALS	Images	Pictures and sculpture.
	Icons	Livery and logos.
	Graphics	Booklets and films.
SYMBOLS	Metaphors	The British lion; the Aussie kangaroo.
	Story	Parable: the fox and the grapes.
	Songs	National anthems.
	Dance	Ballet, jazz, interpretive.

There is nothing new in the idea of communicating a vision through the medium of telling a story. Indeed, it may well be the oldest human communication technique. Stories often have images imbedded within them, but it is the sequencing of events within the story that usually serves to make the tale especially powerful and memorable.

Using stories and images can add considerably to managerial effectiveness but might smack, in the eyes of some people, of propaganda techniques or brain washing or, at a less extreme level, of control, simply unfair persuasion. Such dangers are, in our estimation, usually more illusory than real but it is worth reflecting that the power that comes from using a highly effective communication technique will always need to be balanced against the responsibility of using them with care, thought and essential humanity.

Your vision and the images that go with it are unlikely to be the same ones that inspire and enthuse others. This is not an excuse for retreat into ground that will ultimately reflect the lowest common denominator! You will need to stick to the vision and your own ways of expressing it, explaining what it is and why it works for you so that you listen to alternative perspectives. These will either encourage you to keep what you have or allow your vision to grow and develop. At the end of the day, your vision is your own way of sharing something personal and meaningful. As you link and share more and more work-related issues into your vision it will grow and come to be a part of what others identify as uniquely you.

What a Vision is Not

It is easier to amplify the points made so far by addressing the other side of the coin. It might be easy to conclude from all that we have said so far that a vision is some sort of magic salve to soothe all organisational ills. This is not the case and for every well-known success there may be a dozen failures. No matter how well formulated, a vision can fail if it is inappropriate or if it is poorly communicated or implemented. Sometimes visions fail because right from the very outset they were too ambitious or unrealistic. In a world of change even visions can be overtaken by events and become outmoded before they can be put into action.

For a balanced view of what vision can and cannot accomplish it is useful to be aware of what vision is not. Nanus (1992) has provided a list of points which seem of value:

- Although a vision addresses the future, it is not a prophecy (although after the fact it may seem so). Although there have been visions so powerful that those who first offered them seem in retrospect to be prophets. For example, take Cecil Rhodes' vision of a link between Cairo and the Cape or J. F. Kennedy's vision of an American walking on the moon by the turn of the 1960s. Such visions had power because of the way they captured the imagination of others, mobilised resources and reshaped the reality of their times.
- A vision is not a mission. The organisation's mission is a statement of its purpose not its direction or its sense of destiny. As joint authors of this book we both share the mission of bringing it to print. However, our visions could be radically different: A vehicle for direct change, a contribution to the literature, a source of self-aggrandisement? This is a very simple example of the point, we will have more to say about mission later in this chapter.
- A vision is not factual. It is always about 'tomorrow' and is never likely to have actual concrete existence in the way it was first envisaged. It deals with future possibilities that express hope, dreams, important endeavours and aspirations and these sometimes sit a little uncomfortably with our usual liking in organisations for facts, data and objectivity. This should mean, however, that a vision does not have real substance. Because it may be about future hope rather than present fact, it will still need to be well-informed and relevant to the audience to whom the vision will be addressed.
- A vision cannot be true or false in absolute terms. It can only be weighed in the scales against other directions proposed or intended for the organisation. It could, therefore, be seen as better or worse, engaging or boring, humorous or solid, or in any other comparative terms but not, and this is to repeat the key point, as an unequivocal judgement of worth.

- A vision should not be one-off, static and stated once and for all time. Perhaps one of the problems for NASA with Kennedy's initial vision was what to do next as they came close to the vision becoming a reality. The formulation of new visions needs to be seen as a continuing process and one that is the central role of the driving alliance.
- A vision is not constraining. It is designed to release and direct energy rather than bottle it up and restrain it. There may be occasions when energy has to be funnelled away from directions that are not consistent with the vision, but otherwise a vision is all about direction, origination, opportunities and generally acting as the catalyst for long-term organisational success.

Although a vision is not a mission this is not to understate the importance of forming and using mission statements. The vision must stand on its own as a source of inspiration and direction. A vision establishes a clear sense of purpose, direction and desired future and when widely shared, as Bennis and Nanus remind us, individuals are transformed from robots blindly following instructions into human beings engaged in a creative purposeful venture.

A mission statement is a complementary statement, much less visionary but nevertheless still of value in shaping the organisation's future. In the next section we will examine what we know about mission statements.

MISSION STATEMENTS: THE BOTTOM LINE

Research by John Pearce and Fred David reported in the *Academy of Management Executive* journal (1987) gives some clues to the form and content of corporate mission statements. These researchers examined mission statements from organisations drawn from *Fortune* 500 companies. They discovered that there were eight specific component parts which characterised the majority of mission statements.

- Philosophy.
- Self-concept.

- Public image.
- Customer/market.
- Product/service.
- Geographic domain.
- Technology.
- Concern for survival.

Company Philosophy

A company's philosophy is its basic beliefs, values, aspirations, and philosophical priorities. More than three-quarters (79%) of the respondents included clear indicators of their firm's strategic operating and human resources philosophies. Several did so by attaching elaborate statements of philosophy to more product/market-orientated statements. The following brief excerpts from two statements provide a sense of how philosophies were embedded in the mission statements:

> We believe human development to be the worthiest of the goals of civilisation and independence to be the superior condition for nurturing growth in the capabilities of people.
>
> (Sun Company)

> It's all part of the Mary Kay philosophy – a philosophy based on the golden rule. A spirit of sharing and caring where people give cheerfully of their time, knowledge, and experience.
>
> (Mary Kay Cosmetics)

COMPANY SELF-CONCEPT

Self-concept is an explanation of what the firm's see as their competitive strengths. Seventy-seven percent of responding companies included a description of their corporate self-concept in their mission statement. Hoover Universal and Crown Zellerbach stated the following:

Hoover Universal is a diversified, multi-industry corporation with strong manufacturing capabilities, entrepreneurial policies, and individual business unit autonomy.

Crown Zellerbach is committed to leapfrogging competition within 1000 days by unleashing the constructive and creative abilities and energies of each of its employees.

DESIRED PUBLIC IMAGE

In 87% of mission statements returned, firms expressed their desired public image, making it the second-most included component. Among the ways in which desired public images were expressed were the following statements from Dow Chemical, Sun Company, and Pfizer:

> To share the world's obligation for the protection of the environment.
>
> (Dow Chemical)

> Also, we must be responsive to the broader concerns of the public including especially the general desire for improvement in the quality of life, equal opportunity for all, and the constructive use of natural resources.
>
> (Sun Company)

> . . . to contribute to the economic strength of society and function as a good corporate citizen on a local, state, and national basis in all countries in which we do business.
>
> (Pfizer)

Target Customers and Markets

Altogether 48% of mission statements specified the firm's intended major customer or market targets. The main reasons given for more firms not doing so were:

- specifying certain groups might unintentionally signal 'no interest' to others;
- merger and acquisition activity might violate any predetermined definition of customers or markets; and

- the various markets of many diverse business units effectively dictated a worldwide corporate market focus, and limiting that focus in any way could be confusing to some readers acquainted with smaller markets for individual product lines.

From the mission statements of Johnson & Johnson and CENEX came these clear commitments to specific customer groups:

> We believe our first responsibility is to the doctors, nurses, and patients, to mothers and all others who use our products and services.
>
> (Johnson & Johnson)
>
> . . . to anticipate and meet market needs of farmers, ranchers and rural communities within North America.
>
> (CENEX)

Principal Products or Services

A solid 67% of firms' mission statements were unequivocal in specifying commitment to major products or services. Consider the following excerpts from the mission statements from AMAX and Standard Oil Company of Indiana, respectively:

> AMAX's principal products are molybdenum, coal, iron ore, copper, lead, zinc, petroleum and natural gas, potash, phosphates, nickel, tungsten, silver, gold, and magnesium.
>
> Standard Oil Company (Indiana) is in business to find and produce crude oil, natural gas and natural gas liquids; to manufacture high quality products useful to society from these raw materials; and to distribute and market those products and to provide dependable related services to the consuming public at reasonable prices.

Geographic Domain

For many respondents it was seen as unnecessary to state the 'obvious' global nature of their marketing efforts, which accounts for the fact that only 41% of them specified the intended geographic domain for marketing. Exemplary statements that included this component were the following by Corning Glass and Blockway:

> We are dedicated to the total success of Corning Glass Works as a worldwide competitor.

> Our emphasis is on North American markets, although global opportunities will be explored.

> (Blockway)

Core Technologies

Only 20% of the 61 mission statements evaluated described the firms' core technologies. The principal reasons for omission given by company spokespersons were:

- The impossibility of succinctly describing the many technologies on which their multiple products depended.
- The inappropriateness of trying to describe the core technologies of their service-based business units. Two of the corporations providing noteworthy exceptions were Control Data and NASHUA, which clearly specified their core technologies:

> Control Data is in the business of applying micro-electronics and computer technology in two general areas: computer-related hardware; and computer-enhancing services, which include computation, information, education and finance.

> The common technology in these areas relates to discrete particle coatings.

> (NASHUA)

CONCERN FOR SURVIVAL, GROWTH, AND PROFITABILITY

This was overwhelmingly the most popular component of mission statements with 90% of them stating commitment to survival, profitability and growth, including statements at least as explicit as the following excerpts from Hoover Universal and McGraw-Hill:

> In this respect, the company will conduct its operations prudently, and will provide the profits and growth which will assure Hoover's ultimate success.

> To serve the worldwide need for knowledge at a fair profit by gathering, evaluating, producing, and distributing valuable information in a way that benefits our customers, employees, authors, investors, and our society.
>
> (McGraw-Hill)

THE RELATIONSHIP BETWEEN COMPONENTS AND THE BOTTOM LINE

Systematic analysis of the relationship between these eight components and company bottom line performance is illustrated in the Figure 5.1. The sample of companies (61) was divided into two sub-samples. A high performing group was defined as being in the top quartile of profit margin of all responding companies, the low performers were in the lower quartile.

Statistical analysis reveals that three components of philosophy, self-concept and public image are associated with a firm's financial performance.

It seems clear to us that organisations need both visions and mission statements. The two issues are discrete with perhaps a strong element of overlap between them. The vision must be inspirational and something that 'grabs' the attention of all. The process of turning that attention into ideas for action gives us, in effect, a mission statement.

It does not surprise us that the most significant factors from the Pearce and David study are those aspects of mission that are most general and most likely to be formed from visionary antecedents whilst the least significant are those that speak to fairly specific issues such as technology or survival. Thus the answer to the question 'Does an organisation need a vision or a mission statement?' has to be 'Yes. It needs both along with a realisation that neither is

	Component	High performers' mean score[a]	Low performers' mean score[a]	Statistical difference between mean scores[b]
1	Philosophy	0.89	0.60	Yes
2	Self-concept	0.89	0.53	Yes
3	Public image	1.00	0.73	Yes
4	Customer/market	0.47	0.60	No
5	Product/service	0.57	0.86	No
6	Geographic domain	0.42	0.33	No
7	Technology	0.15	0.06	No
8	Concern for survival	0.95	0.86	No

[a] High performers were firms in the top quartile of a profit margin distribution of all responding *Fortune* 500 companies. Low performers were the lower quartile firms.
[b] A 'Yes' indicates a *t*-value significant at less than 0.05.

Figure 5.1 Corporate mission statement: the bottom line (from Pearce & David, 1987). Reprinted by permission of the copyright holders, Sage Publications, Inc.

enduring or cast in stone.' As the vision becomes closer to specification in terms that allow it to be used as a mission then both will need redefinition.

We have seen, all too often, visions and mission statements produced by organisational wordsmiths rather than the people who have the ultimate responsibility for turning the fine words into actual deeds. The members of the driving alliance will see the impossibility of making anything happen without them standing directly over it unless all the employees they are seeking to influence know what is expected of them in general or specific terms. It will be for the driving alliance to produce, elaborate, revise and update the vision and mission statements. They will also, whenever possible, show by their own behaviour that these are guides to live by rather than mild exhortations which can be framed for hanging in the reception area and then conveniently overlooked.

> Write the vision, and make it plain upon tables, that he may run that readeth it.
>
> (Habakkuk Ch. 2, v. 2)

Nothing in organisational life starts without a history and a context. How things get done will grow from the way 'we do things around here', a brief working definition of what organisational theorists call organisational culture, and thus the logical subject matter for our next chapter.

Chapter Six
CULTURE . . . THE WAY WE DO THINGS AROUND HERE

INTRODUCTION

Culture is one of those nice general words that most people use without stopping to give a lot of thought to exactly what it might mean. To sound profound in any organisation you need only say something like 'Well, of course, it is really a communication problem' or 'Yes, but the problem is buried deep within the history and culture of the organisation' and the chances are that many people will nod and move the conversation along without realising that giving a problem a general label doesn't do much to define, develop or generate workable solutions.

Many psychologists are uncomfortable with the word 'culture', seeing it as having 'been borrowed from anthropology, where there is no consensus on its meaning'. Smircich (1983). Indeed, in more general terms there are some seemingly pretentious definitions of culture that are summed in the popular jibe at our antipodean cousins that 'culture is what yoghurt has and Australians do not' or the more ominous words often (if wrongly) attributed to Goering:

> Whenever I hear the word 'culture' . . . I release the safety-catch on my pistol
>
> Hanns Johst (1933)

The wide diversity of academic and theoretical approaches was nicely summed up by Douglas (1982) when he jammed his tongue firmly in his cheek and wrote:

> Culture is a blank space, a highly respected, empty pigeonhole. Economists call it 'tastes' and leave it severely alone. Most philosophers ignore it – to their own loss. Marxists treat it obliquely as ideology or superstructure. Psychologists avoid it by concentrating on child subjects. Historians bend it any way they like. Most believe it matters, especially travel agents.

This may not be entirely fair and one psychologist, Schein (1985), has taken a broader perspective and given us the most widely used and easy-to-understand model of organisational culture. This is shown as Figure 6.1 as an onion-like model with basic assumptions lying at the core. Here we have the most basic belief and assumptions that underlie the behaviour of the people who work for an organisation.

Norms are the shared sense that a group has of what is 'right' and 'wrong'. Values determine the definition of 'good' and 'bad'. The outer level gives us the more explicit view of what might be going on at a lower level. When we enter the marbled hall of a prestigious financial institution or the grubby reception of a garage, we do

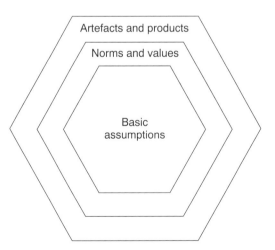

Figure 6.1 The concentric relationship of the components of culture.

not initially say to ourselves 'what an interesting set of values these people seem to have', we have to unpeel the onion, layer by layer.

The model is based upon a formal definition which is a little lengthy but, nevertheless, worth quoting in its entirety. Schein viewed culture as:

> the pattern of basic assumptions that a given group has invented, discovered or developed in learning to cope with its problems of external adaptation and internal integration and that have worked well enough to be considered valid and, therefore, to be taught to new members as the correct way to perceive, think and feel in relation to these problems.

The issue of organisational culture, defined in these terms, has long been recognised. Elton Mayo's Hawthorne studies (Roethlisberger & Dickson, 1939) demonstrated how, in the Bank Wiring Room, a group of employees were able to use sophisticated methods to keep productivity within limits defined by existing cultural norms. More recently, the 1980s saw the publication of a number of books which focused attention on the idea of corporate culture. Indeed, Peters and Waterman's (1982) *In Search of Excellence* became a bestseller. Pascale and Athos (1981) *The Art of Japanese Management* was scanned by many managers for lessons about how to harness cultural differences to improve organisational performance although such a quest, like any designed to find 'the best way' of doing something has ultimately turned out to be a little naive.

How we feel when walking through the doors into an organisation for the first time is probably for each of us an abiding memory. Like the thrill of receiving the very first pay packet. Most of us can remember the gentle shock of realisation that what we took for granted in one set of circumstances is not shared by our new co-workers. Where you sit, how you cope with supervisors, what is an acceptable amount of time to shave off a meal break are all lessons we had to learn to tell us that 'this is how we do things around here'. As Trompenaars (1993) put it:

> Culture is like gravity, you do not experience it until you jump six feet into the air.

Every organisation, large or small, has its culture. Indeed, large organisations may have sub-units, each of which has a culture of its own. The people inside the system are never fully conscious of that culture as a whole or of its parts. There are individual differences in awareness. One employee takes a pride in his occupation (*I'm a time-served engineer!*) while another takes pride in being part of a particular organisation (*I work for One Coat Paints!*).

THE ELEMENTS OF ORGANISATIONAL CULTURE

We can now look in more depth at five overlapping and interacting categories.

- Tradition.
- Beliefs.
- Values.
- Standards or norms.
- Patterns of behaviour.

Tradition

Core assumptions do not spring into existence from a vacuum. They have a history and this past lives on in the organisation's present. This will include the stories, the critical historical incidents, the myths, the founders, the heroes and heroines, the exploits and the folklore, still alive and affecting the system. In an insurance company the founder's portrait is displayed prominently in the board room and his name, vision and acumen are still talked about. That he ruled with an iron hand, made unilateral decisions that adversely affected the lives of many of his staff and ultimately came near to driving the company to disaster are facts that have generally been forgotten. From time to time historical perceptions are officially revised for political and ideological reasons. When Beria was executed for treason, Russian encyclopaedias had to hastily expand their entry for the Bering Strait from one paragraph to three pages to cover the gap that would otherwise have appeared in each volume after he became 'a non-person'.

History lives on in the oral tradition, the stories and myths that are told and retold. More significantly, it lives on because it is embedded in the beliefs, values and norms of the system.

Beliefs

Beliefs, assumptions, understandings and dogma relate to the business, the work it does, the people in it and the environment. Churches state their beliefs explicitly. Some human-service systems espouse many beliefs – for instance, a belief in the dignity and worth of each individual human being, but only a few organisations state their beliefs. However, the trend is changing. The Johnson and Johnson Company has, for example, an elaborate 'credo' that begins 'We believe that our first responsibility is to our customers . . .' This company's espoused beliefs are spelled out explicitly in this statement of philosophy. (For more about company philosophy, see Chapter Five: Vision.)

Values

Values are whatever the organisation prizes. Staff members of a community care centre may prize such things as self-responsibility, honesty, openness, caring, 'tough love', team work, neighbourhood development, personal freedom and fairness in transactions among themselves and dealings with clients. The research presented by Peters and Waterman, mentioned earlier, suggested that the best organisations are those that are 'value driven'.

Norms and Standards

These are the 'oughts', 'shoulds', 'musts', 'dos', 'don'ts', norms, standards, policies, rules, principles, regulations, laws and taboos that govern the behaviour of the organisation as a whole, of the sub-units within it and of individual members of the system.

Ethical standards for many practitioners are published by professional associations and regulatory bodies which specify norms and policies for dealing with clients. Norms and standards spell out the behaviours that will be rewarded in the system and set limits to the kinds of behaviour that will be tolerated.

Patterns of Behaviour

In the system, specific patterns of behaviour, habits, rites, rituals, and ceremonies are prevalent. Just as history and tradition help to mould an organisation's present beliefs, values and standards, so beliefs, values and standards generate the patterns of behaviour prevalent in the organisation. Conservative organisations, for example, prize stability and discourage risk-taking behaviours.

In practice, the development of culture is not a simple one-way process – from history to beliefs to values to norms and thence to patterns of behaviour. Changing beliefs can lead to changes in the ways in which organisation members understand the history. Alternatively, new behaviours may be tried that lead to revisions in the 'oughts' of the system.

To summarise then, both within organisations and individuals, past experiences and behaviours give rise to beliefs, values and norms which are expressed in patterns of behaviour. The ways in which these five interactive categories are patterned constitute the culture of the system.

OVERT AND COVERT CULTURES

Overt Culture

Some aspects of the culture of an organisation may be visible and easily seen by all. Some or all of the five elements may be written down in public documents, discussed in a public forum, celebrated publicly and open to challenge, at least within the organisation.

Some organisations have an official history, honour the date and circumstances of their foundation, have mission statements that outline their beliefs and values, publish policies and rules, have public rituals such as awards, Christmas parties and retirement presentations. All of these are part of the overt culture of the organisation.

Covert Culture

Covert cultural issues are a little like the nine-tenths of the iceberg that remain under water. They represent the degree to which any of the five elements are not written down, only partly understood and remain for the most part undiscussed in public within an organisation.

Kotter and Heskett (1992) have taken the 'iceberg' analogy and extended it. They pointed out that the culture in an organisation has both visible and invisible dimensions and that these are linked to the ease with which cultural change can be brought about.

At the most superficial level we find behaviour common to the large majority of employees that clearly reflects the culture of their employing organisation. Most of us are aware of these, wondering at times how some organisations manage to instil a strong and commonly held sense of the need to respond to customer requests. It is likely that the very visibility of such behaviours tends to sustain them. In the language of the learning theorist they become self-reinforcing. Group norms have long been known as being particularly potent in encouraging enduring ways of working and groups tend to operate sanctions against individuals who do not conform.

Group norms and the ways individuals convey these to each other are usually easy to observe and, if necessary, confront. However, much less visible concerns will be correspondingly more difficult to change. At the deeper level of values there will be important goals and concerns which are less often put into words but which may nevertheless be very important and persistent. For example, not the behaviour that indicates recognition of the importance of the customer but an actual sense of really caring about them. The distinction between the overt and visible aspects of culture and the harder to change less visible aspects is useful in allowing us to recognise that the culture in a business enterprise is not the same thing as a firm's strategy or structure. These terms, along with others such as 'vision' and 'mission' are sometimes used interchangeably because they all play an important part in shaping people's behaviour. If strategy is simply seen as a logic for how to achieve movement in some direction then it has only a partial overlap with all that is better called culture. The similarity exists only for as long as the culture and strategy are in agreement of what needs to be done.

At the deepest levels of invisibility may be issues which are undiscussed or even regarded as undiscussable. Most of us are aware from within aspects of our own family lives that there may be issues which are so sensitive that they are best not talked about. Keeping such issues as a form of taboo may help maintain the status quo but, in cultural terms, prevent more effective discussion or action from taking place.

Some authors have gone so far as to suggest that cultural change may flow best from attempts to grapple with such taboo subjects and bring them into the open. Others argue, from studying a number of what they called 'corporate tragedies', that thinking about the unthinkable is absolutely vital if a business is to be in a position to cope effectively with sudden, unexpected or critical events. They see the important word here as being 'coping'. It might not be possible to prevent all tragedies from occurring, thinking the unthinkable prior to its happening, enables preparation of alternative scenarios. The four kinds of possible 'tragedy' or 'worse-case scenario' that might need to be faced, however unpleasant, might be:

- External malicious tampering with products, 'the evil without'. In 1982 eight innocent people died when the Tylenol capsules they had taken turned out to have been impregnated by an injection of cyanide. The parent company, Johnson and Johnson were forced to recall 31 million bottles of Tylenol with a retail value of over $100 million.
- Harmful defects, the 'evil from within'. In 1980, Proctor and Gamble was forced to withdraw Rely tampons from the market

because of their totally unexpected but nevertheless clear association with death from toxic shock. No one to this day knows why the products 'caused' toxic shock death and the product was removed because of its 'association' with death rather than as a 'cause' but, even so, it cost P&G a $75 million loss on the Rely business.

- Unwanted compatibility, 'the evil of the parasite'. Imagine the horror in the Atari company when it was found that someone had produced an 'adult' game cartridge called Custer's Revenge that would only work on their video games system that showed the hero dodging obstacles to finally be allowed to have intercourse (or rape as many outraged groups saw it) with a bound Indian squaw.
- Projection, 'the evil in the mind's eye'. Sears Roebuck, America's largest retailer, was accused of being in league with the devil on a TV programme because the first three numbers on the company credit card was 666 and this, according to certain religious groups, is the number by which the devil shall be recognised.

It may be hard enough to protect a product from a psychopath armed with a hypodermic but how much harder must it be to protect it from strange and unusual thoughts? The point here, of course, is that unless we are prepared to confront the taboos and 'think about the unthinkable' we run the risk of perpetuating a culture that will be overtaken by changing events in the world outside.

The Tylenol tragedy was widely predicted to be the end of the brand name, but by 1983 the product had regained most of its market share. The company that made it had a strong culture that allowed it to handle the tragedy effectively and bring about changes for the better. Other organisations may have equally strong cultures, but ones that use their normative and value systems to reject the need for change until almost swamped by events. The problems faced by the investors or 'names' in the Lloyd's insurance market represent an example of this. We can think of culture as being 'the tune to which we are all marching'. We will not know, however, just by listening to the tune, if we are marching to success or straight over a cliff!

CHANGING ORGANISATIONAL CULTURE

We need to recognise, right from the start, that this is an issue that continues to be the focus of heated debate and discussion. Many management 'gurus' take it as read that culture change is a necessary part of improving organisational effectiveness, and, by implication, not a terribly hard thing to do. A single example from James A. Belasco's book *Teaching the Elephant to Dance* (1990) will suffice:

> Culture is it. People listen carefully to the messages sent by the Pied Piper of culture. Shape the culture to empower people to use your vision.

Many people see the issues as more complicated. Researchers with a more obviously sociological background who see culture as a socially constructed system of shared beliefs and values seem to find it almost distasteful to think of systematically managing or trying to control the phenomenon. Weick (1983) stated:

> Organisations don't have cultures, they are cultures, and that is why they are so difficult to change.

Other researchers particularly those who search for ways of controlling and improving organisational management are generally more hopeful without suggesting that the task of effecting culture change is an easy one. Indeed, if we see culture as being the 'glue' that holds human organisations together, then change is guaranteed not to be easy.

For example, Warren Wilhelm (1992), sees the best way of starting to change an organisation's culture as being to bring the behaviour of individuals into line with corporate strategy. He offers a 10-point model to improving organisational capability (Figure 6.2).

Although there is much that is useful here, the idea of continual learning to maintain adaptability and the need to align behaviour making what people say, and what they actually do, congruent one with another, are particularly important. However, the rolling together of strategic issues, culture and visioning may be leading to general statements which, while admirable in themselves, do not

- Formulate corporate strategy corporate strategy

- Formulate complementary human resource strategies

- Alignment – communicate the vision, strategies and values

- Assess learning needs

- Provide learning opportunities

- Assess learning results

- Provide more learning opportunities

- Model desired behaviours

- Reward desired behaviours

- Constantly reinforce behaviour change

Figure 6.2 Steps to increase organisational capability (from Wilhelm, 1992). Reprinted by permission of the copyright holders, Sage Publications, Inc.

really grapple with the key issues of how a culture can or should be changed.

Kilman et al (1988) offer a more precise way forward by suggesting that we concentrate on norms and gaps between the culture we have and the one we would like. Their model has five points:

- Bring actual norms to the surface. Identify the behaviour anticipated and expected by a group of its members.
- Articulate new directions. What changes are needed for organisational success?
- Establish new norms.
- Identify culture gaps.
- Close culture gaps.

Allen and Pilnick (1973) have taken the idea of a gap between positive and negative norms even further. Figure 6.3 shows their categorisation of the norms that need to be addressed if an organisation is to move in a 'desired' direction. Some fairly obvious caveats need to be entered. Norms represent tradition and the longer they have lasted the more difficult they will be to change. The idea of there being a single 'good' or 'desired' direction may not always be valid. It seems more sensible to view the norms as issues that need to be kept under constant review if an organisation is to ready itself for planned change or cope with a sudden external crisis along the lines discussed earlier in this chapter.

Additional research has shown that:

- Corporate culture can have a significant impact on a firm's long-term economic performance. Firms with cultures that emphasised all the key stakeholders and leadership from managers at all levels, outperformed firms that did not have those cultural traits. Over an 11 year period, the former increased revenues by an average of 682% versus 166% for the latter, expanded their work forces by 282% versus 36%, grew their stock prices by 901% versus 74% and improved their net incomes by 756% versus 1%.
- Corporate culture will probably be an even more important factor in determining the success or failure of firms in the next decade. Performance-degrading cultures have a negative financial impact for a number of reasons, the most significant being their tendency to inhibit firms from adopting needed strategic or tactical changes. In a world that is changing at an ever-increasing rate, one would predict that unadaptive cultures will have an even larger negative financial impact in the coming decade.
- Corporate cultures that inhibit strong long-term financial performance are not rare; they develop easily, even in firms that are full of reason-able and intelligent people. Cultures that encourage inappropriate behaviour and inhibit change to more appropriate strategies tend to emerge slowly and quietly over a period of years, usually when firms are performing well. Once these cultures exist, they can be enormously difficult to change. They are often invisible to the people involved because they help support the existing power structure in the firm and for many other reasons.
- Although tough to change, corporate culture can be made more performance enhancing. Such change is complex, takes time and requires leadership, which is something quite different from even excellent management. That leadership must be guided by a

realistic vision of what kinds of cultures enhance performance – a vision that is currently hard to find in either the business community or the literature on culture.

FUNCTIONAL AND DYSFUNCTIONAL CULTURES

Even if we accept the idea that the term culture will always be a bit vague and ill-defined, unlike the more superficial and tangible aspects of organisations, it is still important to consider what makes a culture good or bad, adaptive or dysfunctional. Wallach (1983) provides a summary of what cultures do for the organisation:

> There are no good or bad cultures, per se. A culture is good-effective if it reinforces the mission, purposes and strategies of the organisation. It can be an asset or a liability. Strong cultural norms make an organisation efficient. Everyone knows what's important and how things are done. To be effective, the culture must not only be efficient, but appropriate to the needs of the business, company, and the employees.

Why does one organisation have a very adaptive culture while another has a culture that reflects only the past? Is one a case of good fortune and the other a result of bad luck? On the contrary, it seems that any organisation can find itself with an outdated culture if its culture is not explicitly managed.

If left alone, a culture eventually becomes dysfunctional. Human fear, insecurity, oversensitivity, dependency, and paranoia seem to take over unless a concerted effort to establish an adaptive culture is undertaken. It is easy to become scared about what pain or hurt will be inflicted in the future, even in a relatively non-threatening situation. As a result, people cope by protecting themselves, by being cautious, by minimising their risks, by going along with a culture that builds protective barriers around work units and around the whole organisation.

A dysfunctional culture also helps explain some of the self-defeating behaviours that have been observed in many organisations, behaviours that persist in spite of their many disruptive effects.

These behaviours include doing the minimum to get by, purposely resisting or even sabotaging innovation, and being generally negative about the organisation's capacity to change. Worse yet, behaviours may even include lying, cheating, intimidating, harassing and hurting others. While these behaviours may seem unthinkable, they often do receive cultural support even though they cause difficult problems for the organisation. They also significantly undermine both morale and performance.

Dysfunctional Cultures – Some Headlines

As we have suggested, cultures are dysfunctional when they inhibit the people in an organisation from achieving their vision, purposes or strategies. Typically people in such organisations describe in private conversation a variety of behaviour and feelings about themselves and others which are characterised by fear. Peter Block (1987) in *The Empowered Manager*, suggests that employees operate with tacit agreement to requirements such as:

- Submitting blindly to authority.
- Denying self-expression.
- Sacrificing for unnamed future rewards.
- Believing that these requirements are just.

Block illuminates the chilling costs for organisations when they operate with such tacit agreements.

> The price the organisation pays for giving such emphasis to authority is the feeling of helplessness it creates. 'If it's not my fault, I can't fix it.' This is the collusion between management and the people working for them. Managers take comfort in the fact that there are people under their control who are forced to submit to their wishes, and this gives them the illusion of power and influence.
>
> Subordinates take comfort in the fact that when things go wrong, it is not their fault: and the fact that they pay for this comfort with their own helplessness is a small price to pay.
>
> Block (1987)

What People Don't Talk About – The Undiscussables

What are employees afraid to talk about? What is the substance of their fears that lead to feelings of helplessness and to a non-adaptive dysfunctional culture? It is clear that such undiscussables represent a barrier to doing quality work and to building an effective work relationship.

Ryan and Oestreich (1991), focusing on just this issue, identified management practices as the single largest category of undiscussables in the workplace. It includes a variety of issues related to how managers behave. People commented generally about managerial performance, about the technical competence of their bosses and about the way in which their superiors managed people. Other aspects of management practices which were identified as undiscussable were:

- Decision making.
- Favouritism.
- Boss's role in promotions, assignments, etc.
- Information flow.
- Ethics.
- Distribution of workload.
- Politics and power.

These represented the largest single category of undiscussables.

What Are The Behaviours That May Induce Fear?

What contributes to an issue that is undiscussable is the behaviour of managers that may induce fear. Such behaviours were listed by Ryan and Oestreich. They included:

- Silence.
- Brevity or abruptness.
- Snubbing or ignoring people.
- Insults or put-downs.
- Blaming or discrediting.
- Aggressive controlling manners.

Norms of:	Positive norms indicate:	Negative norms indicate:
Organisational and personal pride	That 'company problems are our problems'	'What do I care? I only work here'
Performance/excellence	A success orientation	An acceptance of 'good enough'
Teamwork/communication	That communication is open and two way; people go out of their way to help out	Destructive conflict and unnecessary competition between individuals, groups and departments
Leadership and supervision	That leaders and supervisors are concerned with people and productivity, and act as helpers and standard setters	That leaders and supervisors see their primary role as one of checking and policing their subordinates
Profitability and cost effectiveness	That people see a connection between profits and their well being as employees	That opportunities for cost savings or increased sales are overlooked or neglected
Colleagues or associate relations	The fact that people work hard to see that all colleagues are treated with dignity and respect; that the relationships between the company and its employees is a mutually beneficial and satisfying one	That the company and its employees tend to look at each other as having separate interests and little mutual concern

Customer and consumer relations	That employees see customer satisfaction as the key to personal and organisation success	That the customer and consumer tend to be looked upon as a kind of unavoidable burden
Honesty and security	That security regulations are taken seriously; people place a high value on their own integrity and support such integrity in others	That people are careless or dishonest with company money or products and neglectful in following or enforcing security practices
Training and development	That training and development are looked upon as an integral part of all that occurs within the organisation rather than being confined to separate and formal programmes	That training is seen as unimportant and barely related to the day to day job functioning
Innovation and change	That people are eager to consider new and innovative approaches to solving problems	That people look at new ways of doing things with unwarranted suspicion and mistrust

Figure 6.3 Norm clusters (from Allen & Pilnick, 1973).

- Threats about the job.
- Shouting.
- Angry outbursts.
- Ambiguous behaviours such as behind-closed-door huddles.
- Lack of, or indirect, communication.
- Inconsistency or mixed messages.
- Uninviting behaviours such as not acknowledging folks when they pass in the corridor.
- Unethical conduct.

At root, what lies behind most of these problems is a lack of trust between managers, supervisors and employees. Each side, one suspects, assumes that the other operates from a philosophy of self-interest. Each is expected to try to achieve its self-interest at the expense of the other party. This assumption clearly does not control all workplace interactions. In practical terms, bosses and workers must trust each other to some extent for the work to get done. But as we have pointed out before, trust is historical and even in the most positive of relationships there may exist underlying doubts and concerns which may surface rapidly in times of crisis, change or uncertainty.

Cultures based upon fear and mistrust, on control and helplessness are cultures which induce self-protection. Individuals act in ways which promote their protection, groups become risk averse, managers feel embattled, their survival becomes dominant in their thinking, the customers' needs become subordinate to internal structures, procedures and personalities. These cultures tend to be bureaucratic, not very creative, information does not flow quickly and there is a widespread managerial emphasis on command and control.

An Adaptive Culture

An adaptive culture, by contrast, is described by Kilman et al (1988) in this way:

> An adaptive culture is one which entails a risk-taking, trusting and proactive approach to organisational life. Members actively support

one another's effort to identify problems and implement workable solutions. There is a shared feeling of confidence; members believe that they can effectively manage whatever new problems and opportunities will come their way. There is widespread enthusiasm, a spirit of doing whatever it takes to achieve organisational success. The members are receptive of change and innovation.

Research conducted by Kotter and Heskett (1992) in 22 companies (12 high performing and 10 low performing) tended to confirm, given the constraints of their methodology, Kilman's description. The researchers concluded that in firms with more adaptive cultures, the cultural ideal is that the dynamic alliance initiates change in strategies and tactics whenever necessary to satisfy the legitimate interests of not just shareholders, or customers, or employees, but all three. In short, to build change to meet the needs of a balanced scorecard. In less adaptive cultures, the norm is that managers behave cautiously and politically to protect or advance themselves, their product, or their immediate work groups.

Kilman, Kotter and Hesketh all provide compelling rhetoric for the choice of an adaptive culture. Who would not wish, in the best of all possible worlds, for an organisation dedicated to change, renewal and widespread enthusiasm? Our contention is however still more compelling. Which business today can be without such a culture? We know of no business so protected from its external environment that it could afford to ignore such a compromise.

We have noted elsewhere in this book the teeming complexity of stakeholders who hold expectations (both legitimate and illegitimate) of every organisation. We have illustrated in Chapter Two the impact of changes in US foreign policy upon the bottom-line performance of British Airways in the late 1980s. The directors of that company, without forewarning, were faced with unexpected and unpredicted turbulence so strong that it threatened momentarily the very credibility of a magnificent turnaround prospect. We suggest that no enterprise today, however apparently competent, efficient and dedicated, can allow itself to be sucked into a spiral of complacency which could deny the impact of the unpredictable.

Our business leadership, in these closing years of the millennium, cannot claim to have a crystal ball that will ensure their survival or that of their owners, their customers or their employees. No cohort of strategic MBAs will protect them from events so unpredictable. Indeed, some suggest that the only truly predictable phenomenon is that the unpredictable will occur. Even if that were not the case, the changing needs and choices available to customers, the rising and more precise demands of the financial markets, to say nothing of globalisation of competitive threat, the impact of information technology and the changing aspirations and competency of people at work, demand that leadership must continuously, and with expedition, confront change at every turn,

The need for organisational cultures that are responsive, risk sharing, trusting and proactive are not an optional possibility. Leadership that is doing its job must see such cultures as a requirement of medium- to long-term survival. Furthermore, if we are to believe the Harvard Business School research that this requirement will deliver short-term balance sheet benefits, then our contention becomes even stronger. The time is long since past when well-meaning Chief Executive Officers establish under the guidance of a human resource staff member, a working party of senior executives whose task, within 90 days, is to produce a statement of corporate values which will 'drive the business into the first decade of the next millennium'. Indeed the time is long since past when businesses can afford managers whose principal focus of attention is themselves, who value orderly and risk-reducing lifestyles and who behave insularly, politically and bureaucratically. The time has come to embrace, at the very least, the insights provided by McCall and Lombardo in 1983 about the preferred behaviour of the senior executive.

However, in all of the reading and research that we have completed in preparing this book over the last several years, nowhere have we discovered any writer or guru prepared to disclose how such a culture might be created. Partial insights abound. Magnificent rhetoric is in abundance. Yet nowhere a complete and tested schemata. We know of many, some global, consulting houses which claim such expertise. No doubt proprietary considerations prevent wide-ranging exposure of their methodology!

At the risk of appearing both prescriptive and self-serving we will suggest a way in which it is possible to bring about such a change in culture. Our experience is grounded in the work we began at British Airways in the early 1980s. We have been involved with many subsequent attempts, though it should be said, never with as much position power, nor with as much success.

The Core Values of an Adaptive Culture

An adaptive culture, it has been suggested, is based upon at least six core values and beliefs. Whether this is an accurate number, or whether it might be seven or even only five can be left to the reader to decide from a basis of personal experience, understanding or circumstances. Certainly, we believe that the following six take account of the majority of the variance.

Core Value One – Open and Trusting Relationships

Unless the organisation is characterised by relationships based upon trust, in which people may speak their minds openly, without fear of retribution and in which the concerns of critical stakeholders can be freely debated and issues with these stakeholders can be resolved, there seems little possibility of creating a culture of adaptation. Trust, the glue of organisational functioning, demands that promises, both implicit and explicit, be kept. We have noted earlier in this chapter the risks inherent in dysfunctional cultures. The erosion of trust and openness must be a result. It cannot be mere rhetoric. It is surely not sufficient for senior officers to claim the trust imperative on Tuesday, only to lie, dissemble and break a promise to a customer, colleague or shareholder on Wednesday.

Core Value Two – A Commitment to People

So much has been written on this core value that we hesitate to write still more. Too many organisations in the last 20 years have espoused a belief that 'our people are our most precious asset'. Too many workfolk have experienced the reality of that calumny. Yet the reality remains. No organisation seeking to renew, adapt and respond to a changing turbulent environment could do so without the whole-hearted and driving commitment of its people. There can be no leadership without followers. Followers seek but modest direction; frankness and fairness in relationships and caring for welfare and well-being seem modest requirements. Yet how often do these 'do as you would be done by' needs seem wilfully neglected in so many workplaces today? Commitment to people extends beyond the employment contract. Without a commitment to our people, how can we commit to our customers or our suppliers? We cannot treat our customers better than we treat our folks!

Core Value Three – Participation in Problem Solving Through Teamwork

The role of participation in the workplace, particularly in teamwork, has been long debated. Many millions of pounds have been spent in the development of teams through offsite team-building interventions. The central proposition is that there has to be 'a better way' of ensuring that collections of people, who are joined together in order to achieve a common purpose, can do so with greater efficiency and with greater creativity. The recognition has been based on the widely held and common sense view that 'two (or more) heads are better than one'.

Unfortunately, everyday experience teaches us that the contrary is the more common experience. Groups of people, attempting to solve problems together, often produce camels and not horses. Even so, empirical research since the late 1940s from Bion to the latest work of Jehn and Shah in the *Journal of Personality and Social Psychology* in 1997 would seem to suggest that by the application of some sound basic principles, groups of people can indeed come together and produce more than any single individual could. Adaptive cultures require that groups of work people combine together in imaginative problem solving. Individuals require a sense of belonging to a group that has some control over its near future and in which their views can at the very least be heard.

Core Value Four – A Commitment to Change and Innovation

Turbulence in the external environment requires that the organisation respond, often rapidly, to new and demanding stimuli. The drive to create an adaptive culture is founded on the need for that rapid response. A core value dedicated explicitly to that commitment to change and to innovative change is thus self-evident. To declare that the organisation is not dedicated to the status quo, is constantly pressing for improvement and change, is the first step in the commitment process. The statement of that value implies many subsequent often heart-rending and perhaps very challenging further changes, but the proposition that nothing can be sacred is central to the development of a truly adaptive culture.

Core Value Five – A Commitment to Individual Autonomy

What we seek to express in this core value is the understanding that each individual, provided with and committed to a vision of what the organisation could be, should be given the freedom and autonomy to act in the best interest of the enterprise, without unnecessary let or hindrance. The value attempts to capture the central tenet of the Bennis and Nanus (1985) quotation that individuals gain a sense of importance as they are transformed from 'robots blindly following instructions into human beings engaged in a creative purposeful venture.'

The consequence of a commitment to this value has strong pragmatic outcomes. It is not just soppy woolly-minded rhetoric. An organisation cannot police its entire workforce all the time. There can be no set of rules which cover, for instance, all the circumstances of customer need which present themselves to a BA check-in agent working an eight-hour shift in Terminal Four at Heathrow. That employee must respond intelligently and creatively to each customer's needs, balancing the corporate requirement for speed and value against the customer's needs for accuracy, honesty, empathy and respect. Even when that customer is rude and foul-mouthed or hysterical and frightened. There can be no rulebook for that many human interactions. Autonomy rules OK? Our proposition is simply that once the employee has seen what the organisation can be; they may throw off the yoke of the robot and act in the best interests of themselves, other stakeholders and their enterprise. We ask no less of the check-in agent than we do of the chief executive.

The retail giant Nordstrum in the USA captures the essence of the core value of autonomy in their employee rulebook. It says that the first rule is 'The Customer is Always Right'. There are no other rules!

Core Value Six – An Obsessive Commitment to Loyal Customers

We devoted a large part of Chapter Two of this book to the need to expand the ways in which we might begin to listen to our customers. Meeting with and gathering systematic customer, client and consumer feedback is the first requirement of this core value. Acting non-defensively and then responding constructively to that feedback is the second requirement. Allowing all levels within the business to gather both the data and then to act upon it, within their own sphere of activity, is certainly the third. Finally, a recognition that not all customers at all costs, though not stated directly, is implied in our elaboration of the core-value. No adaptive culture will tolerate the constant abuse of its people or systems by those customers who are not prepared to abide by the reasonable rules associated with honesty and the respect for human dignity. Adaptive cultures require the balancing of the needs of the owner and the staff against the excesses of rude, belligerent, corrupt and inebriated customers. We cite the example here of the US airline that bans customers from flying on its aeroplanes forever if they are rude and/or drunk, in order to protect their staff.

The second step in the development of an adaptive culture is to ask the question 'If we are to subscribe to these six core values, how will we know have to behave?' Critically, the question is not addressed to the entire workforce. It is addressed in the first instance to those at the top of the enterprise who act as the significant role models. Those we have called the driving alliance. Those whose behaviour will have the most pervasive effects on those who they may lead. Culture change is about leadership. Leadership is about culture change.

But leadership is also about defining and acting out the new behaviours. We call these behaviours management practices, not workforce practices. The answer to the question 'How will we know how to behave?' requires patience and precision. Upon the answer rests the success or failure of the culture change process. For each of the core values identified, a list of precise, action-orientated observable behaviours must be articulated. The process of generating such a list may involve widespread consultation amongst all levels of management. It may involve the use of outside consultants. What is certain is that the final listing must state clearly and unequivocally the management practices that will bring to life the core values. In the following chapter we will attempt to help the reader to begin to spell out in greater detail the behaviours that we think best exemplify each value.

Step three in the process involves the widespread communication of the core values and linked management practices. Kotter (1996) suggested that undercommunication by a factor of 100 is often the cause of large-scale change failure. Certainly, undercommunication of the core values will result in failure. In the British Airways case the management practices were communicated to all 2500 key managers by means of a five-day residential training course.

Step four requires that each manager (and for that purpose we might define a manager as any employee who has responsibility for three or more subordinates) receive direct feedback on each of the management practices from employees and from peers and bosses. This feedback should be easy to understand and should be capable of providing each manager with an action plan for change in his/her behaviour. Where managers express the need for follow-up help, guidance and counselling, this should be provided by appropriate human resource backup. The action plan for change should be incorporated into the manager's performance management objectives, carrying the same weight as other key result areas in that contract.

Step five requires that the organisation change those parts of the system which directly contradict the espoused core values of an adaptive culture. For instance, such changes may involve the provision of new ways of defining financial accountability, provision of training, the selection of new team members, the development of budgets or even the way in which the bureaucratic processes of the business may be streamlined. The most obvious of these need to be tackled with determination and haste. Others may be left until individual managers and their work groups can formulate new and more responsive mechanisms for dealing with them. One part of the system that we believe will always be critical to success of the change process is the reward system for management. Our experience suggests that the management of the enterprise must see a clear link between the effort they put in to changing the way they behave and some tangible benefit.

Since the development of the culture will take time, the intrinsic benefits will not be immediately apparent. An appeal to delayed gratification, sometime hence, will be insufficient to sustain the endeavour. In the British Airways case we introduced a performance pay regime which clearly linked behaviour change to a bonus. Not to the exclusion of business performance objectives, but in addition to them. The relationship between these elements (behaviour and business objectives) was multiplicative. Failure to deliver on either element resulted in a zero bonus and the development of a new way of 'doing things around here' was secured. Neither was subordinate to the other. Both required energy and focus. Both were valued equally in the eyes of the most senior executives. Rewards both financial and in terms of advancement were directly linked to building the new culture.

Step six is simply to persist. Persistence and determination alone are omnipotent. There will be many occasions in the following two or so years when belief and patience will be challenged. The gainsayers and lame hearted will spell out the dire consequences of this course of foolishness. The politicians and the weak brained will also see opportunities to subvert the endeavour, and will attempt to do so. Try not to be swayed. Best practice suggests that in the end the strength of the adaptive culture will be worth all these minor tribulations.

Chapter Seven
MANAGEMENT PRACTICES . . . . THE FULCRUM FOR CHANGE

AN INTRODUCTION

In their attempt to provide a model of organisational performance and change, Burke and Litwin (1992) suggested that at least two lines of theorising needed to be explored – organisational functioning and organisational change. In Chapter One we presented the component parts of their model. In that model they suggested that management practices sat clearly at the top of that part of the model called transactional. By contrast, in the Georgiades & Macdonell model also presented in Chapter One, we placed management practices at the centre of the leadership component of transformation. In this chapter we will attempt to explain our reasoning for what is a quite radical change.

Significantly, in our view, in neither of the two papers produced by Burke and Litwin describing their model are we able to divine the *mechanism* by which management practices are determined. In this chapter we will also articulate what we know about how management practices are formulated based upon custom and practice.

Finally this chapter will offer some practical guidance in the determination of the management practices with examples for each of the core values.

MANAGEMENT PRACTICES, TRANSFORMATIONAL OR TRANSACTIONAL?

Burke and Litwin defined management practices as 'what managers do in the normal course of events to use the human and material resources at their disposal to carry out the organisation's *strategy*. By practices we mean a practical cluster of specific behaviours'. In defining management practices in this way Burke and Litwin claimed that they were following the work of such people as Boyatzis (1982) and Luthans (1988).

The present authors do not challenge the integrity either of the definition or the logic of their empiricism. We do, however, challenge the reason for suggesting that management practices are essentially transactional. Undeniably, the way managers behave affects the climate of the work-group. Empirical research has confirmed this commonsense conclusion (Fleishman, 1953). However, included in the Burke and Litwin definition and italicised in their quotation is the word *strategy*. Elsewhere in this book we have taken pains to note that the vision and the culture of any organisation as well as the changes to the vision and to the culture of any organisation are the primary work of a driving alliance of leaders. Therefore, we argue further that, since strategy encompasses the management behaviour necessary to accomplish revised organisation outcomes, it is undeniably the case that at the very least *the specification* of what managers must do in order to accomplish that strategy is transformational.

The task of specifying the significant and required management practices is a visionary task, though their implementation may be essentially tactical and thus transactional. The specification, we believe, may be a 'consensual task'. It must certainly be the task of all members of the driving alliance who collaborate together to define the new organisational vision.

Our experience would further suggest that the specification of management practices is simply not enough. Transformational failure, though not noted by Kotter in his 1995 article, is often ascribed to the failure of senior executives who do not practise what they preach. At the very least managers, expected to conform to a new set of management practices designed to carry out and make

WE THE WILLING
LED BY THE UNKNOWING
ARE DOING THE IMPOSSIBLE
FOR THE UNGRATEFUL

WE HAVE DONE SO MUCH
FOR SO LONG
WITH SO LITTLE
WE ARE NOW QUALIFIED
TO DO ANYTHING AND EVERYTHING
FOR NOTHING

Figure 7.1 A common notice board flyer.

real the organisation's strategy, demand honourable rhetoric. Rhetoric which demands in turn, that senior executives behave in the way that they have stipulated others should behave. 'Do as I tell you, not as I do', is no longer acceptable. Such dishonesty gives rise to the proliferation of photocopies of the kind which do the rounds of office notice boards shown in Figure 7.1.

In practice then, the specification and modelling by senior executives of management practices is the fulcrum of organisational transformation. It is axiomatic that in attempting to shape new behaviour, we must provide accurate feedback to all managers about their present behaviour. Further and continuous feedback about their attempts to change their behaviour in the desired strategic direction is also a requirement.

We can illustrate this issue by reference to the example given in Burke and Litwin (1992). They suggested a management practice 'encouraging subordinates to initiate innovative approaches to tasks and projects'. Having specified such a practice, we suggest that two things follow. First, the manager must know how their subordinates perceive their current behaviour. Over the passage of time the manager also needs to know the extent to which his or her behaviour has changed in the desired direction. The implication of this feedback means that some kind of change is implied in the performance management system of the organisation. In many cases it implies the *creation* of a performance management system. Further, it also implies that once the feedback is available, managers should be rewarded for significant endeavour. Such changes to both the performance management system and to the reward system are acknowledgements of transformation and not merely transaction.

The role models for significant organisation transformation are its leaders and its managers. For transformational change to happen it must be as a result of employees experiencing change via their day-to-day contact with their own managers. Only by interaction in this way, with managers who are trying hard to behave in new and different ways 'in order to carry out the organisation's strategy', will individual employees experience the reality of cultural change. There can be no transformation without significant change in the way managers and leaders interact; in the way they do what they do. Not just in what they say they want, nor just in what they say they believe in, but actually in the way they behave. This behaviour is defined and specified in the management practices, aligned with the strategy and enacted and modelled by the leadership.

THE SPECIFICATION OF MANAGEMENT PRACTICES

The starting point for the specification of key management practices is the vision statement and the strategic programme which is aligned with that vision. The vision statement (the statement of the organisation's purpose) should address the needs of the three primary stakeholders of the balanced scorecard:

- owners,
- customers,
- employees.

The culture of the enterprise must be aligned with the strategic imperatives which flow from the needs of these stakeholders. Often, leaders are moved to produce an interim document called a values statement which bridges the vision on the one hand with specific management practices on the other. Figure 7.2 is an illustration of just such a business values statement.

The actual technology for the specification of management practices has developed considerably since the earliest examples of listed management practices which used in a large-scale training exercise in Citicorp Bank in the late 1960s.

Some examples from that organisation can be seen in Figure 7.3. The management practices are expressed in terms of managerial behaviour in the second person singular, i.e. each statement begins with 'you'. This is the earliest example known to the authors. Five domains were identified and the number of practices in each domain varied between six and nine. No public information exists which indicates how these management practices were specified for that organisation.

The earliest example of management practices specification in which the authors were involved was for British Airways in the 1980s. Here two consulting organisations (the Forum Corporation of Boston and the Pilat Consulting Organisation of Tel Aviv and London) collaborated in the production of a set of some 20 management practices which redefined the required managerial behaviour for BA's future. As can be seen in Figure 7.4, four domains were specified, each domain was called a factor, and each factor contained five management practices.

The actual derivation process for the production of the British Airways management practices remains obscure; this is due in part to the lack of clear articulation of the process adopted by the consultants themselves. This, it must be said, may have been due to the need on the part of the consultants to keep their processes proprietary. It is also likely that they too were on a very steep learning curve. What is clear, even with hindsight, is that the actual specification process involved fewer rather than more managers. With hindsight, the extent of participant involvement seemed correct then and still does.

It remains inconceivable to the authors that the process for the

Generation Wholesale Division

Our Business Values

ScottishPower

Our business values are the basic principles upon which our policy is formulated and which govern the management and conduct of all of our business operations. We believe that a clear declaration of these values both to ourselves and to others will assist in the definition of standards of behaviour for everyone and the consistent application of these standards throughout the Division.

The values are supported and reinforced by a series of practices which are the observable commitment to the values. All managers (managers are those individuals who have responsibility for others), are expected to incorporate these practices into their day to day management activity. Although the practices are directed specifically at all managers, the values are for the guidance and direction of all staff in the way that they carry out the work of the Division.

TRUST
We believe that our stakeholders want to deal with an organisation that they can trust, therefore:
- we say what we think and believe to be true.
- we honour our commitments.
- we share our objectives and plans with our stakeholders by expressing them clearly and unambiguously.
- we recognise that mistakes will happen. On occasions when they do the circumstances will be reported fully and accurately.
- we will promote openness and honesty in dealing with all of our stakeholders.

CUSTOMERS AND SUPPLIERS
We believe that business success depends upon us meeting the requirements of our customers and establishing good business relationships with our suppliers at all times, therefore:
- we encourage communication with customers and suppliers, internally and externally, to agree requirements and to develop understanding of changing and dynamic needs.
- customer satisfaction depends upon continuous development and maintenance of our business systems and processes.
- we will continuously develop our relationship with our suppliers in order to gain and sustain competitive advantage.

ENVIRONMENT
We believe that our plant and equipment and other resources must be managed in a way that protects the environment. It is important that our neighbours recognise our commitment to environmental protection, therefore:
- we will be recognised as industry leaders in our appreciation of the environmental impact of our business activities.
- our strategic decisions will be directed at minimising our impact on the environment.
- we will endeavour to gain the respect of our neighbours by demonstrating our commitment to environmental protection and by explaining the complexity of our operations and their impact on the environment.
- we will establish and maintain close and continuous contact with all who may be effected by our operations.

CARE AND DEVELOPMENT OF THE INDIVIDUAL
We recognise that our objectives can only be achieved through the efforts of our people and that their well being and development is essential for continuing success, we believe therefore that:
- individual responsibility and accountability cannot be shared.
- individuals are unique and that we need to listen regularly to them in order to understand and recognise their needs and aspirations.
- each individual should have clear and measurable performance objectives.
- accurate, honest and timely feedback on individual performance, given on a regular basis, improves job performance and communication.
- feedback should recognise and reward achievements and contributions as well as providing corrective guidance.

- roles and responsibilities must be clearly defined, demanding and, where possible, provide variety, challenge and satisfaction.
- training and development are essential for business success and although individuals have the ultimate responsibility for their own development, the business is committed to providing training and development opportunities in accordance with its present and future needs.
- external and internal events will bring about changes in the business and that we will only be able to respond rapidly to these needs through the willingness of individuals to take on new skills and to apply their skills creatively.
- that training and development needs must be discussed regularly with all staff on an individual basis.
- that we must be actively concerned about the well being and welfare of our staff.

TEAMWORK
We believe that teamwork is essential to business success and that membership of an effective team is both satisfying and productive, we are committed therefore to:
- recognising the role of managers in setting the strategic direction for their team.
- creating and supporting natural teams and ensuring that everyone understands their roles and responsibilities in relation to their team.
- encouraging, at all levels, the involvement of team members in decision making and problem solving.
- recognising and rewarding the achievement of teams.
- demonstrating that teamwork is our visible commitment to a partnership with our people that is meaningful and effective.
- recognising that the best possible solutions will be obtained by getting ideas from everyone with something to contribute.

HEALTH AND SAFETY
We are totally committed to managing our plant, equipment and other resources in order to protect the health and safety of our people, contractors and visitors, we will therefore:
- be committed to developing and following rules and procedures that reinforce and reflect the priority given to health and safety.
- support the rules and procedures with good judgement and health and safety training for all staff.
- rigorously promote that safety is part of everyone's job.
- regularly conduct safety audits and act positively to remedy any deficiencies.
- never compromise health and safety in the pursuit of other objectives.

Figure 7.2 The ScottishPower Generation values and management practices.

Getting commitment to goals and standards	You communicate high personal standards informally – in conversation, personal appearance.
	You demonstrate strong personal commitment to, and persistence in, achieving your unit's goals.
Coaching	You build warm, friendly relationships with the people in your work group, rather than remaining cool and impersonal.
	Your staff members can be completely open in telling you about their mistakes.
Appraising performance	You consider all relevant information, when appraising staff members' performance.
	You work with staff members to determine their realistic short-term career objectives.
Compensating and rewarding	You use recognition and praise (aside from pay) to reward excellent performance.
	You are more likely to recognise staff members for good performance than to criticise them for performance problems.
Managing a staff for continuity of performance	The work group meetings you conduct serve to increase trust and mutual respect among work group members.
	You periodically try to get a feel for work group morale.

Figure 7.3 Some examples taken from Citicorp's managing people practices

specification of key management practices should be determined by a large number of managers. This was certainly true in the case of British Airways because the required transformation came about as the result of wide-ranging and long-lasting organisational inertia. Thirty years of public-sector managing is not a breeding ground for managerial development and managers often 'do not know what they do not know'. Perhaps more critically, few managers could conceive of the possibilities and the requirements of a radical set of management practices.

THE MENU OF PRACTICES

FACTOR I
CLARITY AND HELPFULNESS

FACTOR II
PROMOTING ACHIEVEMENT

Establishing clear, specific objectives for subordinates.

Emphasising and demonstrating commitment to achieving goals.

Helping subordinates to understand how their jobs contribute to the overall success of the organisation.

Giving subordinates feedback on how they are doing.

Clearly defining standards of excellence required for job performance.

Communicating your views to others honestly and directly about their performance.

Providing help, training and guidance for subordinates.

Recognising people more often than criticising them.

Giving subordinates a clear-cut decision when they need one.

Recognising subordinates for innovation and calculated risk taking.

FACTOR III
INFLUENCING THROUGH
PERSONAL EXCELLENCE AND
TEAMWORK

FACTOR IV
CARE AND TRUST

Knowing and being able to explain to others the mission of the organisation and how it relates to their jobs.

Behaving in a way that leads others to trust you.

Communicating high personal standards informally through appearance and dedication.

Building warm, friendly relationships.

Noticing and showing appreciation for extra effort.

Paying close attention to what people are saying.

Sharing power in the interest of achieving overall organisation objectives.

Responding non-defensively when others disagree with your views.

Willing to make tough decisions in implementing corporate strategy.

Making sure that there is a frank and open exchange at work group meetings.

Figure 7.4 The four factor menu of practices used in British Airways in 1984–85.

Thus, in the British Airways example, a number (30 or so) of in-depth interviews were undertaken. The intent of the interviews was to spell out the implicit values and expectations of those key 'actors' at the top of the business. From these interviews the consultants derived a list of the management practices required in order to bring about the significant and required behaviour change. The list is shown in Figure 7.4.

These management practices formed the core of feedback given to each manager during a five-day training programme 'Managing People First' and was the basis for a significant part of a complex new performance management programme.

More recently the technology of management practices specification has been made more transparent. Working from the value statement already shown for ScottishPower (Figure 7.2) which was a critical part of the process, the management practices shown in Figure 7.5 were derived. The procedure for the specification was as follows:

1. Twenty in-depth interviews were conducted with senior executives of the division.
2. Consultants examined in depth both the vision and strategic planning documents in order to identify key implicit values. At the same time staff attitude survey results were examined in order to confirm or reject these value hypotheses.
3. The implicit values derived from step 2 were used to list as many likely management practices which related to each value as possible. A comprehensive library of some 600 management practices was developed, cross-referenced to some 50 value statements.
4. These likely management practices were then presented to a wider sample of key managers in the organisation in questionnaire form. Each manager was asked to rank each management practice as to its importance.
5. The results of the questionnaire were presented to a senior management workshop involving the top 15 managers in the division who produced both Figure 7.2 on business values and the management practices associated with these values illustrated in Figure 7.5. The two-day workshop focused almost entirely on the results of the questionnaire study and on resolving conflicts in these data.
6. One hundred and sixty managers in the organisation received feedback on each management practice from a minimum of three subordinates. The feedback was delivered during a five-day leadership workshop.

Trust

My manager keeps his/her promises.

My manager shares key information with me.

My manager is open and honest in dealing with me.

My manager is consistent in his/her plans and actions.

My manager takes time to build a supportive relationship with me.

My manager explains how changes in the wider business world affect our business decisions.

Care and development of the individual

My manager agrees clear performance objectives with me.

My manager provides me with honest, accurate feedback about my performance.

My manager gives me guidance, counselling and training to help improve my performance.

My manager recognises (praises) my good performance.

My manager involves me in planning my own career development.

My manager is concerned with my welfare and well being.

Teamwork

My manager listens and is open to ideas that differ from his/her own.

My manager encourages frank and open discussions at team meetings.

My manager defines the strategic direction of our team.

My manager helps me to understand the role of our team in the wider organisation.

My manager helps define our team goals and each team member's role and responsibilities.

My manager holds regular team meetings.

My manager encourages us all to become involved in problem solving and decision making.

Customers and suppliers

My manager talks regularly with our customers.

My manager talks regularly with our suppliers.

My manager promotes quality and continuous improvement in everything he/she does.

My manager develops and implements more efficient and effective ways of satisfying our customers.

My manager sets standards and goals in agreement with our customers and suppliers.

Environment

My manager complies with agreed environmental standards in establishing strategic objectives.

My manager acts in ways that limit the effects of our business on the environment.

My manager maintains close, regular contact with those who may be affected environmentally by our operations.

My manager shares his/her understanding of environmental issues with everyone that he/she meets.

My manager encourages us to implement new ways of working to minimise our impact on the environment.

Health and safety

My manager provides health and safety training for me.

My manager conducts regular safety audits.

My manager provides us with feedback on all safety audits.

My manager does not compromise on issues of health and safety.

My manager involves me in reviewing health and safety rules and procedures.

My manager emphasises my responsibility for my own health and safety when reviewing my performance.

Figure 7.5 The six factors and management practices of ScottishPower Generation wholesale division 1991–92.

THE SIX CORE VALUES OF AN ADAPTIVE CULTURE AND THEIR MANAGEMENT PRACTICES

In the years that have passed since the British Airways and ScottishPower values and practices were gathered we have been able to garner additional data from a range of other organisations. The lists of management practices that have emerged have reflected specific factors that are of particular, perhaps even unique, importance to one organisation but not to another. These specific factors aside, we have also been able to see the development of a set of values and practices which are more general in that they cover many different enterprises and industries. In the section that follows we will outline the management practices linked to the six core values associated with the adaptive culture identified in the previous chapter.

We present both some management practices for each core value and some notes and advice on each practice. We make no apology for moving from what has been a rather intellectual argument to a level that gets us as close to coaching and counselling as is possible through the medium of the printed page. Both are important and linked. The cerebral issues of how to bring about effective organisational change can only be translated into profitable results by having the right people doing the right things. We have obtained great personal pleasure by being able to offer individual managers specific hints and guidance notes to assist them in determining what they personally were going to do when they returned to their 'back home' workplace. We would be failing in our stated aim if we did not try to offer as much direct advice as possible.

Core Value One – Open and Trusting Relationships

If we do not remain open to the widest variety and range of inputs then we will appear to be only motivated by narrow functional concerns, by valuing self-interest over organisational interest or appearing to keep others at arm's length rather than allowing them to influence us in the way we seem to want to be influencing them. Trust stems, in a very important way, from our day-to-day attitudes and actions. If we are honest and open with others, if we take a risk and let them know when we disagree, if we make every effort to support rather than subvert, we will be respected and trusted by colleagues throughout the organisation. We will also be more influential.

'Trust' is a word with numerous emotional connotations and vague associations. Trust and openness are frequently linked with the notion of honesty but although you and I may 'know' that we are essentially honest we may appear to others to be untrustworthy. This might be due to the fact that we have a reserved personality. Perhaps because we have to keep something unsaid as a result of our commitments to others who trust us to respect their confidences. In any event, we need to be careful not to see a seeming lack of trust-worthiness as equating to deceitfulness or dishonesty. In business relationships trust is more often synonymous with:

- Dependability
- Consistency
- Predictability
- Reliability

When people talk about trust they most often talk about one of three components: information, judgement and execution.

Trust of Someone's Information

- Is it timely?
- Is it accurate and unbiased?
- Is advice given in the best interest of the receiver?

Trust of Someone's Judgement

- Do I understand this person's decision process or does it appear off-hand?
- Do I get conflicting signals (for example, does this person make jokes about the values they claim to espouse)?
- Does this person talk about others behind their backs?

Trust of Someone's Execution

- Does this person do what they say they will do?
- Can I count on this person to tell me if an agreed commitment cannot be met?
- Does this person keep confidential information confidential?

Trust is fragile. It takes a long time to build and only a moment to destroy. Trust is most evident in its absence. Behaviour that might lead others to distrust you includes:

- Errors of omission (forgetting a meeting, not listening).
- Errors of commission (damning with faint praise behind someone's back).
- Inconsistency (rapidly changing behaviour on returning from a training course).

Trust is the glue that holds teams together. When it is present, time is saved, decisions are reached more quickly, the flow of ideas and move towards consensus are hastened and the process leads to enhanced effectiveness.

Here are some suggested behaviours that subordinates, managers and peers might expect to see if the values are being 'lived'.

Management Practices Associated with Open and Trusting Relationships

A manager keeps promises and commitments, does not play politics

- Builds a reputation for standing by the commitments that have been made.
- Ensures consistency between plans and actions.
- Does not agree to anything that cannot be sanctioned.
- Refuses to do anything simply because it enhances own standing or status.
- Lets people know as soon as possible if unable to keep a commitment.

A manager shares key information with subordinates

- Gives the whole story. Does not let information out in small packets.
- Answers follow-up questions immediately or strives to get the extra information.
- Does not give different people different parts of the story.
- Gets key points delivered ahead of 'the grapevine'.
- Strives to be accurate and reliable when passing on information.

A manager is honest; never dissembles

- Gives advice in the best interest of the receiver.
- Is consistent and dependable.
- Behaves in the way he or she would expect from others.
- Sets organisational interest above self-interest.
- Lets you know when he or she disagrees with you.

A manager builds supportive relationships with peers, subordinates and bosses

- Obtains information before offering opinions or suggestions.
- Will not appear unduly deferential or dominant.
- Offers help without immediately expecting something in return.
- Does not express glee at other's misfortune.
- Talks about 'our' problems not 'yours' or 'theirs'.

A manager shows no favouritism

- Does not assume others got ahead because of an 'inside track'.
- Emphasises objective criteria for reward and advancement.
- Acknowledges and appreciates extra effort.
- Acknowledges the unique skills and talents of others.
- Shares important information.

A manager is warm and friendly

- Examines the nature of interactions with staff.
- Doesn't send contradictory messages.
- Gives positive feedback for self development as well as for good performance.

- Is prepared to engage in non-work-related conversations when appropriate.

Core Value Two – A Commitment to People

Maintaining the highest standards of customer service and improving productivity will never be easy. Nothing can happen unless we are capable of taking our people with us in ways that show our real commitment to them as individuals. Giving them a 'sense' of our commitment is shallow and ultimately counter-productive if we show for even a second that the 'sense' is superficial and artificial and that beneath the surface we have no real commitment to them as human beings.

One of the most direct and obvious ways you provide 'strokes' for staff members is by recognition that they did a good job. This form of behaviour reinforces good performance and encourages the staff member to repeat what went well.

Positive feedback about performance can be given in four ways:

- Direct recognition. Give a subordinate a direct compliment for good performance.
- Earshot. Tell someone else about a subordinate's performance so that he or she overhears you but always be careful about this strategy; it can have negative implications for issues to do with trust.
- Third-party recognition. Encourage someone else to offer recognition for good performance.
- Formal recognition. A response for good work where suitable praise is mentioned in memos, at staff meetings, in personnel files, etc.

Showing commitment to people comes as much from listening to them as it does from doing things to, with or for them. Managers who show they are listening rather than just appearing impassive have been shown to be more successful than those who appear to have been occupied with other thoughts and concerns.

Managers are often called upon to play roles that are a little to one side of the conventional 'boss–subordinate' relationship and act in ways that demonstrate a willingness to pass on accumulated experience or be more active in sponsoring the interests of subordinates, making sure they have a fair share of opportunities and perhaps even protecting them when the unexpected means that their endeavours are not all crowned by success. These activities are sometimes all grouped under the heading of 'mentoring'. Whether the word is used with its connotation of a more personal commitment to individuals than would be embraced, for example, by the term 'coaching and counselling' is probably a matter of individual preference.

There can be no requirement that managers and subordinates must be, in any conventional sense of the word, 'friends'. Indeed there are times when to be so can produce significant problems. What is required, however, is the recognition that subordinates will expect, and have a right to expect, a minimum level of frank, honest and direct feedback from managers and a basic concern for their health, safety and, in more general terms, what are sometimes called 'hygiene needs'.

Again, here are some guidelines expressed as suggested tactics:

Management Practices Associated with a Commitment to People

A manager is concerned with welfare and well-being of subordinates

- Provides health and safety training for me.
- Does not compromise on issues of health and safety.
- Listens to problems when there is a need to talk through.
- Is prepared to go as far as he or she can to balance work and personal dilemmas.
- Asks about feelings and seems genuinely interested in the answer.

A manager encourages frank and open discussions about subordinates' performance

- Prepares for appraisals. Marshals an array of positive and less positive feedback material.
- Initiates real discussion and does not simply run through a checklist of rehearsed points.
- Is prepared to listen to reasons for failure and mitigating factors with an open mind.

- Asks questions and listens to answers.
- Follows up on agreed remedial action.

A manager agrees clear performance objectives

- Negotiates targets rather than imposing them.
- Will not allow targets to be set impossibly high or too low.
- Ensures workloads are evenly balanced.
- Accepts the possible impact that the external environment might have had on previous poor performance.
- Is prepared to accept his or her own share of any blame for missed targets.

A manager demands honest, accurate performance

- Encourages subordinates to realise why success or failure has occurred.
- Quantifies performance outcomes in realistic ways whenever possible.
- Consults widely for personal feedback to use.
- Refuses to accept easy or superficial reasons for success or failure.
- Does not punish people for honest efforts that failed.

A manager gives guidance, counselling and training to improve subordinates' performance

- Simplifies complex issues into ones that are manageable.
- Makes self accessible to people who need guidance and support.
- Regularly reviews training plans with staff.
- Thinks flexibly and creatively when setting goals for staff.
- Offers ideas and suggestions rather than firm advice.

A manager involves and encourages subordinates in their own career development

- Asks probing questions about development needs even when subordinates do not ask for help.
- Acts as a sounding board when necessary.
- Finds opportunities to stretch people and move away from their comfort zones.

- Is willing to allow secondments, shadowing and project work to widen opportunities.
- Encourages involvement with professional bodies, external working parties and committees.

Core Value Three – Participation in Problem-Solving through Teamwork

Participation sometimes raises a dilemma in the minds of managers who know they are skilled, competent and able to do most of the important jobs in a section or department. Arranging to have things done by others takes time, involves awkward human things like feelings, sensitivities and emotions and takes infinitely longer than if you just sat down and did them yourself. However, and here come the horns of this particular dilemma, there is never enough time to be able to do everything on one's own and, even if you could, there would certainly not be enough time for trying different or new things. So, participating and getting things done, with, by, and through the medium of others is at the very least a necessary evil.

It can, of course, be more than this. The summed knowledge and experience of a group of people when properly marshalled and applied can lead to outcomes which are successful, creative and innovative in a way that would have been far beyond the initial comprehension of any single member of the group. The requirement of a manager is therefore how to avoid the unnecessary delay and friction of getting people to work together and encouraging participation which uses the sum of all the contributions to produce a result greater than the individual parts.

The manager is not required to be the most active, vocal, dynamic or busy member of a group. Participation does not equate to energy or volume of work. It is rather that a manager must operate as the conductor of the subordinates' orchestra, knowing when to introduce one person's ideas and when to keep another silent. There are many roles that subordinates and managers can play and this is not the time or place to elaborate team types or similar approaches. The interested manager can find these easily elsewhere. For the purposes of giving feedback to improve the effectiveness of subordinates a manager will need to make a careful distinction between two types of possible actions that might suggest themselves as being appropriate:

Content behaviour. Acting as a member of the team or group to contribute ideas, information, suggestions or anything that aids the group to achieve its objective.

Process behaviour. Looking as a group member, from the inside out, at what is going on within the group. Is everyone contributing? Are some people dominating? Is there an air of friendly acceptance of each other or is hostility crackling around the table?

Few managers have much difficulty with the first of these. Indeed, one of the reasons they were often promoted to a managerial position was for the very reason that they were good at them in the first place. The providing of feedback to subordinates places much greater weight upon the second and more difficult approach. The need to attend, at one and the same time, to both content and process is in itself a difficult task but anyone concerned with improving participation has no choice other than to try. The best way forward is often to let the initial logic of task accomplishment provide the first set of guidelines. Is a group proceeding logically from information to opinion to obtaining a range of suggested solutions and thence to agreement or are different people trying to push forward too quickly? Less obvious to see are the issues of group climate that might be at work. Are people generally supportive, willing to recognise good work by others and capable of using a joke to deflect unpleasantness or are there levels of tension and disagreement that are acting to undermine and spoil the task-related progress that may be being made?

It is not the manager's job to recognise and act on all of these but it is his or her duty to make sure that someone is. Participation is related to the skills of being a team member as much as being either a manager or a subordinate.

Management Practices Associated with Participation in Problem-Solving

A manager helps the team to understand their role in the wider organisation

- Gets people to act as substitutes in important meetings.

- Encourages visits and liaison meetings.
- Calls in 'experts' from other functions to explain any unclear indices or requirements.
- Sets face clearly against inter-departmental rivalry which causes friction rather than healthy competition.
- Ensures that press cuttings, releases or statements are circulated quickly.

A manager encourages the team to define team goals

- Constantly questions the need for meetings.
- Vocalises objectives at the outset of any meeting.
- Allows individuals to further shape and refine goals as they work rather than insisting they be done later.
- Gets the team's view on excellence and how to achieve it.
- Encourages competition between, not within, teams.

A manager encourages the team members to define individual roles and responsibilities

- Establishes clear individual objectives.
- Maximises individual potential by giving key people stretching tasks but without reducing morale.
- Holds people accountable for the achievement of key results.
- Is willing to listen to requests for reallocation of tasks or resources.
- Prevents individuals from becoming stereotyped.

A manager encourages frank and open discussion about the way the team works

- Asks probing questions when others seem reluctant to participate.
- Asks about how the group worked rather than just about results achieved.
- Finds out what everyone thinks and not just what the more vociferous have to say.
- Does not shirk from the idea that he or she may not be behaving optimally within the group.
- Keeps asking 'so what do we do to make it better next time?'

A manager listens and is open to ideas that differ from his or her own

- Avoids saying 'yes – but . . .'
- Checks understanding of all that has been suggested before responding.
- Goes away and thinks about suggestions before saying no or offering an alternative view.
- Gives open acknowledgement of new ideas even if they are not acted on or subsequently modified.
- Criticises ideas in a way that does not imply personal criticism of the person who generated the idea.

A manager encourages the team to become involved in problem solving

- Knows when to include others in solving problems.
- Helps members visualise links and relationships between issues.
- Provides an encouraging climate by words and gestures within which problem solving can take place.
- Provides recognition for high level achievement.
- Makes a special effort to celebrate and applaud success.

Core Value Four – A Commitment to Change and Innovation

This value reflects an issue we have visited several times in the development of our ideas. Leadership is about stimulating change and innovation while management is about controlling and integrating what happens. The 'trick' therefore for management practices will be the recognition of when inevitable change (probably something driven by the demands of the external environment) must be implemented by careful management control and when, on the other hand, the status quo is becoming too stultifying and failing to recognise subtle or potential shifts in customer requirements. Thus, new ways of doing things must be 'kick started'.

The manager often finds it uncomfortable to have to stand at the boundary between those people who are screaming for change and those who are clinging for dear life to old, comfortable and secure ways of doing things.

Increasingly the inevitability of change is percolating through most organisations. Resistance to change becomes increasingly weary resignation that life will always be lived in a state of flux and chaos. Managers who can encourage their staff members to at least embrace the idea of looking for new and better ways of doing things will find that such management practices may bring double benefits. The first is fairly obviously that better outcomes may actually result! The second is that at the very least obstructive attitudes and a need to 'hang on by the finger tips' will be seen as counter-productive. Few people today need an explanation of the oft-quoted managerial maxim 'If you are not part of the solution you must be part of the problem'.

The behavioural science literature has addressed the topic of resistance to change since the 1940s. The techniques needed for the development of effective management practices will spring more from releasing what is inherent than by trying to impose behaviour from outside. Most people fear change because of the consequences they have experienced in the past or fear in the future. Dealing with these is generally the way to change. There is some evidence to suggest that groups who do not have the internal resources to be innovative and gather new ideas may need to have someone 'planted' within the group to help with the task but our own experience has been that most teams actually have the capacity if only the right behaviours are encouraged and rewarded.

Management Practices Associated with Change and Innovation

A manager informs subordinates about corporate imperatives and initiatives

- Passes material on quickly; does not 'sit on it'.
- Anticipates 'what does it mean to us?' questions.
- Encourages staff to share their perspectives, hopes and fears about what is happening.
- Trades in facts and data and stamps on wild rumours.
- Brings senior managers to meetings to elaborate when necessary.

A manager constantly responds to customer feedback

- Accepts positive feedback and does not rationalise negative feedback as being due to the errors of others.
- Responds to immediate problems with immediate actions.
- Does not lose customers without asking them why they are taking their business elsewhere.
- Tries to understand what the customer really wants. Is not quick to say 'what we usually do is . . .'
- Makes sure that key customers get the most immediate attention.

A manager encourages subordinates to try out new ideas

- Rewards and praises attempts to try new ideas.
- Does not give marks out of ten for new ideas. Implements them or says why it is not being done now.
- Is willing to allow time and 'pump-priming' resources to try new things.
- Becomes personally associated with new approaches, does not wait to see that they are successful first.
- Helps foresee broader questions or potential roadblocks and offers help to deal with them.

A manager exposes subordinates to best people, best ideas and best practice

- Shares contacts.
- Finds out which competitors are 'best in class'. Encourages staff to find out why they are not equally good.
- Shows personal unwillingness to put up with second-class service from own internal and external suppliers.
- Runs informal workshops or discussion groups spontaneously when given an unexpected opportunity or visitor.
- Encourages investigatory trips, visits or fact-finding activity that leads to new insights.

A manager ceaselessly asks and pushes others to ask questions about performance

- Keeps re-visiting and updating performance objectives

- Updates goals as circumstances change.
- Uses a range of measures to evaluate long-term as well as day-to-day success or failure.
- Never seems comfortable with the status quo. Always looking for new ways of doing things.
- Makes it clear that 'doing more of the same' is not valued or likely to be rewarded.

A manager loves learning, reads widely and attends training

- Is enthused by new ideas, techniques and developments.
- Asks questions of anyone who might be able to teach him or her something.
- Has a personal development plan which includes learning goals.
- Makes time to attend training events.
- Keeps abreast of current affairs with particular reference to own discipline, industry and competitors.

Core Value Five – A Commitment to Individual Autonomy

'There can be no learning without error.' Every parent as well as every manager faces the problem of how far you allow individual growth and freedom, but organised in such a way that prevents errors from being too disastrous, damaging or permanent.

The management practices which best address this area are more to do with the managing of perceptions than the actual management of subordinates' behaviour. The manager will need to ensure that there is no initial ambiguity of objectives or targets. Once this has been made clear it will be the individual's self-perception that comes most obviously into play. Once subordinates have learned the habits of being successful and rewarded for doing 'the right thing' they will come to expect that they will be able to continue to 'do right'. This expectation will encourage a form of powerful and enduring self-assurance. If, however, early experience is negatively rewarded, or simply punished, then we should not be surprised if people learn behaviours which stop them from being hurt, ignored or disciplined rather than doing things that are risky and which might not work.

The management practices that revolve around individual autonomy are concerned with shaping the environment for individuals rather than 'doing things' to people.

Management Practices Associated with A Commitment to Individual Autonomy

A manager gives authority to act and make decisions without upward reference

- Does not expect detailed plans and advance notification of work schedules.
- Expects individuals to monitor their own timekeeping.
- Always gives initial support to a subordinate's decision even if subsequent modification seems needed.
- Makes a particular point of praising individual initiatives.
- Negotiates boundaries of authority when necessary rather than imposing them in advance.

A manager encourages others to act in ways that promote the best interests of the business

- Allows others to make any needed sensible commitment to a customer.
- Does not shrink from hearing unpleasant news.
- Emphasises the needs of all stakeholders not just 'ours'.
- Encourages long-term quality not short-term expediency.
- Does not fight to hold a team together if releasing people or responsibility gives wider gain.

A manager cuts through unnecessary red tape

- Allows anyone to question the need for any form of 'chitty'.
- Will not countersign anything purely out of habit or as routine.
- Does not stand obviously on ceremony or hold status more important than function.

- Understands which systems are important for safety and security and which are likely to be redundant.
- Confronts inefficient systems rather than learning ways to get around them.

A manager encourages problem solving not problem stating

- When given a problem always asks 'and what do you see as the answer?'
- Allows people to develop unusual solutions to novel problems.
- If presented with a problem and an obvious solution suggests that next time the approach should be to fix it first and inform later.
- Does not allow people to rest content having defined or named a problem. Asks 'what are you going to do?'
- Values informed action but not analysis to the point of paralysis.

A manager ensures appropriate levels of financial authority

- Understands audit trail requirements and questions anything that appears not to fit this.
- Ensures staff have the financial authority to fit the commonsense requirements of what they are doing.
- Actively questions the reasons for any seemingly strange restrictions.
- Values the need for security without doing anything to cast doubt on an individual's honesty.
- Does not treat petty cash or business supplies as personal property.

A manager never punishes error in new endeavour, but asks 'What did you learn?'

- Honestly sees problems as learning opportunities.
- Balances gains and losses when things go wrong and keeps both in perspective.
- Clearly values trying and failing as better than inactivity.
- Offers training, coaching and counselling in an open-minded way.
- Debriefs people involved with error to find out what happened and without a hint of scapegoating.

Core Value Six – An Obsessive Commitment to Loyal Customers

Given the whole tenor of this book there is perhaps little need to say much more about customer orientation than has already been put into Chapters 2 and 6. Management practices will need to reflect the importance of the customer in terms of behaviours rather than general exhortations along the lines of 'The Customer is King!'. This may be true but what do individuals have to do to show this in their behaviour as well as in what they say?

Many employees do not have to be told anything about customers. They spend their lives dealing with them and are only too aware of the fact that their livelihoods and financial security are dependent upon the range of humanity that comes to them for assistance. Others live lives sealed, intentionally or otherwise, from the demands or pressures of customers and may need reminding from time to time of the ultimate importance of continuing to meet customer needs.

Managers are often in something of a cleft stick in having to manage groups that interface directly with customers yet who also have roles that force them to look inwards. Thus, the need for absolute conformity between what managers say and what they do is most critical. The management practices developed to expand this area of customer orientation all reflect this to a greater or lesser extent.

Management Practices Associated with An Obsessive Commitment to Loyal Customers

A manager meets and talks regularly with customers

- Makes time to talk informally with customer groups.
- Performs subordinates' jobs periodically to talk to customers in their own environments.
- Attends gatherings and functions where customers will be present.
- Telephones customers who have written to complain or offer praise for more detailed information.
- Sets up joint working groups to investigate and solve problem issues with customers.

A manager constantly seeks customer feedback

- Initiates surveys of customer opinions.
- Finds ways of using employees as 'listening posts' to get customer feedback.
- Uses the anecdotal experiences of family and friends to assess how well customers are treated.
- Looks for indirect ways of getting customer data – letters to the press, consumer publications, etc.
- Ensures collaborative and two-way relationship with marketing and customer relationship departments.

A manager promotes excellence, as defined by customers, in everything

- Never says 'It will do. They will never notice.'
- Does not take 'It's OK' as an acceptable customer evaluation.
- Wants to know what problems the customer's customers might be experiencing.
- Is willing to lend staff to help develop an improved product.
- Keeps asking 'What could we do better/quicker?'

A manager attempts to predict new, as yet unspoken, customer needs by means of market research

- Is aware of the need to 'intercept' future requirements by planning own R&D to fit anticipated customer developments.
- Uses appropriate techniques to 'guesstimate' future trends.
- Charge employees with the tasks of trying to predict changing trends and anticipating their impact on customers.
- Shares information about general trends, changes and market shifts with customers.
- Sponsors joint research projects with customers and suppliers.

A manager encourages all staff to be involved with customers especially those who have 'defected'

- Ensures that everyone knows how their part of a function ultimately bears upon what the customer buys.

- Encourages everyone to telephone customers at moments when they have a little free time to gather any available feedback.
- Keeps attention concentrated on important customers not just those who are 'nice' or who complain loudly.
- Always asks customers why they took their business elsewhere even if everyone says 'We already know why'.
- Encourages staff and colleagues to use, if appropriate, and comment upon customers' products.

A manager is never defensive in the face of customer criticism

- Listens with respect and an honest effort to understand an angry customer's point of view.
- Offers solutions not excuses.
- Does not rationalise or try to shift blame to other departments.
- Tries to produce an explanation and, if appropriate, an apology, even if the business has already been lost.
- Ensures that everyone knows that fixing problems quickly and efficiently actually contributes to customer loyalty.

FORMS OF FEEDBACK

Without feedback there can be no learning. It is worth pausing for a moment and thinking about the full implication of this statement. It is sensible to take every possible precaution to prevent error, but without the opportunity to make mistakes we will not give ourselves or others the chance to increase the store of our knowledge and skills. Many people are happy to rely upon dual-control cars with qualified instructors when their offspring learn to drive, but seem to expect subordinates to learn and develop without much more than a quiet 'word to the wise'. Feedback is not a synonym for praise, a 'wigging', performance appraisal or a reading of the riot act. If subordinates are to behave in ways that play their part in leading and managing organisational change, then they will need a constant supply of feedback from as many sources as possible.

Feedback is information about performance that leads to action for changing or maintaining performance. There are two kinds of feedback – motivational and formative. To give feedback to staff effectively a manager should understand that each form of feedback has a very different purpose.

Motivational feedback tells the person what he or she did well and rewards him or her for it. Its purpose is to encourage the person and to reinforce his or her behaviour by pointing out the good performance.

Formative feedback tells the person what needs to be done better and how to do it. Its purpose is to help the person see how he or she could do a better job the next time.

Splitting the Feedback

The separation or 'splitting' of these two forms of feedback is very important. By giving only motivational feedback immediately following a staff member's performance, you allow him or her to gain confidence: that is, to feel good about his or her job.

By giving formative feedback at a different time, just before the next performance, you help him/her do things better the next time, which increases his or her competence. Examples of both forms of feedback are given below.

Motivational feedback (immediately after a performance): 'John, you really did well getting this analysis finished so quickly. I know it wasn't easy at such short notice.'

Formative feedback (just before the next performance): 'John, next week is probably going to be very busy; please make sure you leave time to check the customer service data for typing errors.'

If John were to receive the formative feedback and the motivational feedback at the same time, two things probably would happen:

- He wouldn't appreciate the motivational feedback because it would be overshadowed by the more negative content of the formative feedback.
- He probably would forget the formative feedback (about proof-reading) long before the next busy time.

Timing of Feedback

One of the most common beliefs about feedback is that, to be effective, it must be given immediately after a performance is completed. This is generally true for motivational feedback, but formative feedback should be given when the performer has an opportunity to use it.

If formative feedback is given immediately after the act, the performer is likely to forget much of what was said by the time the situation comes up again. Also, formative feedback after a performance is viewed as 'pointing out what I did wrong'. Having your errors pointed out when you can't do anything about them right away is almost always a punishing experience. Therefore, formative feedback needs to be given when it's most likely to be:

- Accepted
- Remembered
- Used

To do this, there are three helpful guidelines for timing formative feedback.

Feedback Guidelines

Give formative feedback as close as possible to the time when the task will be performed again. Instead of giving formative feedback immediately after a staff member's performance, talk to him or her just before he or she repeats the performance. That way, your suggestions will be fresh in his or her mind, and the suggestions will be seen as advice.

Obviously, it's not always possible to give formative feedback immediately before a task is done again. However, you should think ahead to what the staff member will be doing in the coming days or weeks, and decide which type of formative feedback is appropriate.

Give the formative feedback when the staff member is receptive to it; that is, when he or she is interested and attentive. Otherwise, the staff member may simply nod and not absorb your suggestion or demonstration.

A staff member may not be receptive because he or she may:

- Be focusing on another task at the time.
- Be mentally or physically exhausted.
- Be distracted and show evidence of anger, fear, or personal concern.

In other words, give formative feedback when it's convenient for the staff member, not for you. It's better for you to spend a little less time with a staff member when he or she is receptive, than to spend several hours, at your convenience, working with someone who's not really paying attention.

Give formative feedback often enough to prevent too great an error. Otherwise, the staff member may make an error that you could have prevented with proper instruction.

How to Give Feedback

While there are many aspects of giving feedback which could be discussed, we feel there are ten major 'shoulds' which, if followed, can make feedback more constructive and can help to avoid defensive reactions which block communication. These are as follows:

- Perceptions, reactions, and opinions should be presented as such and not as facts.
- Feedback should refer to the relevant performance, behaviour, or outcomes, not the individual as a person.
- Feedback should be in terms of specific, observable behaviour, not general or global.
- When feedback has to be evaluative rather than purely descriptive, it should be in terms of established criteria, probable outcomes, or possible improvement, as opposed to making judgements such as 'good' or 'bad'.
- Feedback regarding an area of performance should include a discussion of what are viewed as the 'high' and 'low' points of that

performance and the specific behaviours which appear to be contributing to or limiting full effectiveness or accomplishment.
- In discussing problem areas in which there are technical or established procedures for achieving solutions, suggestions should be made regarding possible means of improving performance.
- Feedback should avoid 'loaded' terms which produce emotional reactions and raised defences.
- Feedback should be concerned with those things over which an individual can exercise some control, and/or be given in ways which indicate how the feedback can be used for improvement or planning alternative actions.
- When encountering rising defences or emotional reactions, the person giving feedback should deal with these reactions rather than try to convince, reason, or supply additional information.
- Feedback should be given in a manner which communicates acceptance of the receiver as a worthwhile person and of that person's right to be different.

Common Defence Mechanisms to Negative Feedback

The following are common defence mechanisms which we should be aware of and sensitive to when giving feedback:

Blaming others	– 'I did my best, but my team let me down'.
Making excuses	– Claims that external factors prevented us from completing or doing the task properly: 'How could we have got it done on time with all the interruptions we've had?'
Anger	– We get angry when a matter is raised about which we feel sensitive.
Denial	– Refusal to accept the feedback.
Attack	– When we feel accused, we may defend ourselves by launching a counter-attack.
Sulking	– When we feel hurt, we withdraw, refuse to participate in the discussion, avoid eye contact and attempt to make the feedback giver feel guilty.

How to Receive Feedback

Less can be said about receiving feedback than about giving it. However, certain points are worth noting. These are that feedback received is always based on past behaviour – not current or future behaviour – and that receiving feedback always offers the possibility of learning something valuable which can serve as a basis for future improvement.

There are also certain steps to follow in receiving feedback which can increase its value for the receiver. These are as follows:

- Listen carefully.
- Try not to let defences build, but mentally note questions or disagreements.
- Paraphrase what you think you hear to check your perception.
- Ask questions for clarification and ask for examples in those areas which are unclear or in which disagreement exists. Paraphrase answers again.
- Carefully evaluate the accuracy and potential value of what you have heard.
- Collect additional information from other people. Observe your own behaviour and other persons' reactions to it.
- Do not overreact to feedback, but, where desired, modify your behaviour in suggested directions and then evaluate the outcomes.

This has been a long chapter and necessarily so. We make no apologies for the mixture of general reflection and down-to-earth detail that it contains because the issue of management practices is one that is central to a number of themes in our overall approach. We have argued that leadership is a collective responsibility of members of the driving alliance and thus the behaviour they initiate, shape, require and, of most importance in our experience, model, becomes the life blood that flows around the vessels of any model of organisational existence.

We have moved from description and analysis towards prescription and advice. It now seems appropriate to make such steps more obvious and attempt to conclude in a way that does justice to the ideas and the readers' needs to be able to transfer them to their own circumstances and organisations.

Chapter Eight
THE DRIVING ALLIANCE AT WORK

At the beginning of this book we suggested that we were not in the business of writing a step-by-step, painting-by-numbers, guidebook. This was not to be a book of proscribed paths, sights to be seen or meals to be eaten. More likely, we suggested, a book by guides still exploring some complex topography. In this last chapter we will attempt to draw together some threads, first by way of clarification, second by way of preparing our readers for their journey and finally to assist in providing a view of the landscape and not of the litter bin.

It was James McGregor Burns who suggested that it was the prime responsibility of leadership to articulate the dominant contradictions at each turning point in history. Our first lies here. We will find it difficult at times to be less than prescriptive. Our recipes, guidelines, tenets and maxims have, we trust, so far been but gentle common law. Often, in this chapter, we will perforce be moved to provide more firm advice.

THE DRIVING ALLIANCE MEMBERSHIP AND NORMS OF BEHAVIOUR

The driving alliance is not a group of the unwilling, chosen from the unfit, to do the unnecessary. Throughout the preceding chapters we have noted the centrality of the driving leadership alliance to the definition and solution of most, if not all, of the issues raised. We wish now to address directly some issues central to that alliance.

Our position is clearly collectivist. By habit and instinct most of us construe leadership to be singular. We indeed have reviewed what seem like aeons of leadership research, where singular women and men were the object of enquiry. Our driving alliance is essentially plural. Our leadership, the driving alliance, is a collective. Great things are today rarely created by singular individuals. Big ideas do not emerge from the solitary labours of a singular genius. No great organisation change can be achieved by a leader acting in isolation.

Furthermore, the collective is an alliance not a disjunction. Our most common observation for the failure of transformational change within businesses is not, contrary to many other observers, failure to articulate a clear enough set of goals, or death by 1000 initiatives, or even imposing change without sufficient employee involvement, but quite simply that the ruling hegemony could not talk to one another, did not care for one another and certainly did not wish in any way to ally with one another. Senior management teams where 'knighthood centred leadership' or 'I didn't get to where I am today by listening to other people centred leadership' is present are not likely to deliver a driving alliance. This may seem a crude caricature and yet, today, individuals who exemplify these values dominate many businesses.

We have seen the enemy and it is the lack of a driving alliance. Our driving alliance must feel and smell the commitment to the need for change and improvement. They are clear about why they must change and what things will look like when they have succeeded. They are dedicated to balance. Primarily, they are dedicated to the inherent balance of the balanced scorecard. They believe in and will design a process of transformation, where decision making is moved as close to the customer as possible, and where employees are involved in radically different ways, enhancing their working lives and building their commitment and loyalty. At the same time they will help the owner to understand, often delaying gratification to enhance longer-term equity value. These driving alliances speak their minds openly and freely, are not dominated by fear or ignorance, and drive together to achieve a balance of strategy and tactics. You will not find amongst these driving alliances those 'macho-execs' both male and female who sneer at the idea of feelings being central to the argument or who use as a bastion of their critique, statements grounded in the primacy of shareholder value. This driving alliance is not a group who individually can do nothing but as a group decide that nothing can be done. They are committed to one another and are jointly committed to their primary stakeholders.

What if they are not, or cannot be? Our own prescriptions on this issue are straightforward. We must take responsibility for asking the three Ls to find employment elsewhere. These Ls are:

- The Liars, those who have difficulty in confronting the truth, in themselves or in the data and who would prefer to live their organisational lives in a plethora of falsehoods.
- The Lazy, those who 'didn't get to this level in the organisation to miss out on the privileges of rank'. Particularly when these privileges mean golf every Wednesday afternoon, many long weekends and every conceivable boondoggle. They are often found, rarely to be sustained and will be unprepared for the rigours of the journey that you all will face. Ask them to leave early, it saves so much pain later.
- The Lame-hearted, those folks whose cynicism is often cloaked in aged experience. 'We tried that in 1957 and it didn't work then, and it won't work now', or 'You can't teach this old dog any new tricks, she's seen them all'. The lame-hearted are no less pernicious than the other two Ls. They weigh down upon the body politic particularly when in senior slots and make progress a heavy burden.

Even culled of these liabilities the driving alliance must still be wary. The most common and ongoing problem faced is illustrated by the following Jewish folk tale.

Six rabbis, travelling by sea, ended up together in one lifeboat in the midst of a massive storm. Rabbi Levi sitting in the bow of the boat looks aft only to spot Rabbi Cohen making circular motions with his right hand in the bottom of the boat. 'What are you doing?' screamed Levi over the howl of the gale.

'I'm drilling a hole!' was the reply.

'What for you're drilling a hole in the bottom of the lifeboat?'

'Why not? It's my part of the lifeboat.'

Too many people really feel that as functional directors, they own their own directorates. That their part of the lifeboat is subject only to their whim. Let the driving alliance be cautious. These drilling lifeboatmen need to be reminded, at the first symptom, that they are merely temporary custodians and that the well being of the community must not be threatened by their selfish needs for autonomy or glory.

One further word of caution. It has always been a source of astonishment to us, that even the best driving alliance is unaware of its own power and visibility. We have often found it necessary to remind alliances that even though they may meet off-site or only on the senior executive high-security floor, their words and actions, jokes and grimaces are public property. However well protected and shielded by their acolytes, it is as if they live, work and converse inside a glass house with large public address systems perched on each corner broadcasting to the world at large.

There is no invisibility for the members of the alliance. Each action, even the most *sotto voce* conversations are noted and the informal communications network will hum with interpretations, implications and outcomes. The speed of that informal network is often staggering. At British Airways, for instance, we would estimate that an ill-judged remark made by a senior executive on boarding an aeroplane in Asia, would have become part of common parlance by the time the plane landed at Heathrow. The driving alliance is never off stage.

THE DRIVING ALLIANCE: THE FIRST STEPS

Once the driving alliance membership and behavioural norms have been sorted you may be ready to begin the work. Preparation for the journey is vital. Please don't assume that you can just stride out. Before working at any level of detail, make sure that you all agree upon the map. We, of course, would recommend our model as the essential guiding framework. Which map actually used is really less important than a total agreement amongst alliance members that you are all using the same map, and that you all understand at the same level of comprehension what each element of the legend means and its implication for action. If not, spend the time, do the work and allow differences of comprehension and interpretation to surface. Deal with the uncertainty, do not allow any individual's faint heart in the face of ignorance to go unnoticed. We would contend that for every hour spent by the alliance in getting these opening issues clear, a month or more will be saved in the downstream implementation.

Since this team will face the unenviable task of changing the organisation for the future and simultaneously running the organisation in the present, it will be tempting to delegate tasks. Our observation is that ineffective alliances often delegate the future and hang on to the present. Too often we have seen senior teams delegate visioning to task forces or culture change to consultants while clinging like drowning sailors to the minutiae of the daily operational report. Do not abrogate the present, keep quiet control, but drive with all might to the future. There can be no sensible delegation of the central transformational tasks. Making the business better is the central task of the driving alliance. That is what transformation is about. It is not a 'nice to have' flavour of the month, keep up with the CEO-Joneses, project or activity. It is about transforming the business and as such it is not amenable to delegation. Nor is it often going to be a quick fix. Managers are impatient, looking for the quick way round. Driving alliances understand the long-haul and are committed to their destiny. That does not mean that they lack urgency, this is no lacklustre, limp-wristed cabal. But it does mean:

- That they cannot delegate the future.
- That building a resource team to support the endeavour of change does not mean visiting the agenda item once a month.
- They will not get there by close of business on Friday, even though that would be nice.

How long will it take to reach our destiny? In truth, how can one tell? In one sense never. In a more pragmatic sense we can guesstimate that it will take one year's worth of focused change endeavour for every ten years' worth of prior existence. Thus, estimates for the full turnaround of BA in 1983 were between four and five years. The task was just about completed by 1988 in time to begin the second round of transformation.

THE SPECIFICATION OF STEPS: SOME GUIDING PRINCIPLES

Principle One

Start with your customers. Use intelligent and sophisticated mechanisms for understanding their perceptions of you, your product, and your performance. Use the matrix in Chapter Two to ensure that you have covered all the possible ways to collect the data. The data itself will be contradictory if you have not controlled for the issues of focus. Put in place immediately tracking mechanisms for customer feedback. These data are central to the steering of the transformation process. Integrate customer feedback into your balanced scorecard. Build the communication strategy for the entire exercise around the need for change to meet raised customer expectations.

Principle Two

You can't treat your customers better than you treat your folks. Understand where the hearts and minds of your workpeople are. Again, you can use our proprietary instruments but you don't have to. Simply ensure that whoever does the data collection understands the range of methodologies available, knows the meaning of reliability and validity, and doesn't confuse opinions with attitudes. Finally, ask the alliance members the question 'How will we be able to act on the data once we have it in our hands?' If you can't answer the question, rethink the arrangements. Your staff will expect action as a result of any kind of opinion seeking activity and the alliance had better be prepared to drive forward with an action plan once the data are at hand.

While it will not be possible yet to determine the definitive cultural characteristics of the future, the data from the community should answer at least what needs to be discarded from the past. Again if the data collection does not help answer this question, rethink the arrangements.

Finally, do this simple exercise. Review your customer data and check to see whether these issues seem to appear with any regularity in the feedback you are getting.

- Don't ignore me.
- Don't lie to me.
- Make me feel wanted.
- Keep your promises.
- Give me clear information.
- Listen to me when I tell you how to improve your product or service.
- Be sensitive to my needs.
- Treat me fairly, give me value for money.
- Don't make me ill.
- Don't insult my intelligence.
- Don't keep me waiting.
- Encourage my continual use of your product or service.
- Don't rip me off.

Beware, if these are the kinds of things your customers say directly to your face, these will be the issues that you need to confront in the way you manage your business, because this too will be the feedback from your folks. The new culture will have to strive to eliminate these dysfunctional management practices, which probably characterise the current 'way we do things round here'.

Principle Three

With these two sets of data to hand, begin to craft your vision. What could it be like in 20 years' time for your shareholders and owners, for your customers and for your employees?

Remember we think you should be slightly embarrassed by your rhetoric! Don't look upon this activity as a bureaucratic drafting task. This is not just another item on the main board agenda. Let go! Create a new destiny and allow all of the members of the alliance to shape and modify the dream.

Spend many hours on the task. Draft and redraft but don't make it so wordy that you can't explain it to the storekeeper and the janitor in five minutes and see the glistening in their eyes as you finish. This is a dream for your folks and their future, not a document to be scrutinised for due-diligence by a city law firm.

The purpose of the vision is to inspire and to share with the entire community a sense of mutual meaning. The rhetoric requires simplicity and focus, enhanced by analogy, metaphor and stories; very often making explicit some strongly held, but rarely expressed common purpose. We have often been astonished by the extent to which people respond positively to what cynics might call 'corny'. For instance, it was a group of power station manual workers who reminded us that their job was 'keeping the lights of Scotland burning, and the premature baby incubators running'. It was cynical and highly paid PhD economists at the Bank for Reconstruction and Development (the World Bank) who reminded us that despite all the politico-economic jargon of their daily work, their real purpose, the reason that they came to work at all, was the alleviation of poverty and sickness in the Third World. And the customer service workers at British Airways whose campaign slogan became 'Who Serves Wins!' and who described their reason for being as the loving and caring for travellers. Hard to believe that these very same people, three years earlier, would have described travellers as punters and would have hidden from them, in the duty room, given the slightest provocation.

Principle Four

Once crafted the vision must be over-communicated. The process should be taken as seriously as the marketing launch of a new product or service to potential customers. We have noted earlier that the under communication of the vision by a factor of ten (or maybe 100) is a fundamental cause of change programme failure. We really do suggest that you treat it as seriously as you would a new product launch. Insist on using your very best marketing brains and involve the communications competence both in-house and externally. Brief these people carefully and, if necessary, arrange a 'beauty contest shoot-out' between potential external agencies or consultancies. Insist that all techniques be on the table, from poster advertising through other media to below the line activity. For one short period within BA during the People First campaign, every piece of corporate notepaper carried the strap-line, and every employee (including every senior manager) was expected to wear the 'we're putting people first!' lapel badge. Members of staff, approached by the Chief Executive, who were not wearing the tin badge, were offered a replacement which was immediately pinned in place. That simple below-the-line marketing device, soon became a badge of honour. Sir Colin Marshall was never seen without his for two years.

The launch itself requires as much imagination and creativity as your budget will allow. But please don't be condescending. Too often, we have heard, 'Oh, this won't be of any interest to such and such a group or department or class of workers'. The PPF campaign involved, initially, all 20 000-plus customer-service staff, but it was soon extended to all other functions. We're often asked how was it possible to justify the cost. We can't. In direct costs the price per employee for the two-day event was probably less than £20 at 1984 prices. The indirect and opportunity costs we could not calculate. The value of the exercise as a vision launch, with the subsequent downstream impact was immeasurable. British Airways today is the industry standard. It started the process of renewal with PPF.

And the medium is the message. The way you choose to go about marketing the vision will say much about your commitment and the new culture that is implied. Recently we heard of a CEO who instructed that the vision and values statement for the company be issued only to the top 300 managers. They were then to be invited to a two-hour seminar (non-compulsory) for a brief explanation. It was not wise, he argued, to require any further involvement for fear that this activity might get in the way of the already heavy workload. Close scrutiny of the values statement revealed a massive change in the dominant culture, and the cynicism about the commitment of the CEO to the perceived much-needed change was immediate.

Principle Five

Culture is where it is at. However good the mechanism for the delivery of operational or customer service improvement may be, insufficient attention to the adaptive culture of the enterprise will probably be the ultimate cause of the meltdown of your efforts. We are aware that to outsiders, and to some insiders, culture change is outmoded. The very act of talking with precision about what we stand for or believe in is unfashionable and often unacceptable. The cost of the disruption inherent in the change is incalculable. The imposition of new cultural norms is often seen as a suppression of the different, the creative and the innovative. Blah! Blah! We have probably heard every excuse devised by man (and woman) about why 'changing our culture would not be right for us'. These reasons usually come from the top of the business, and give little cognisance to those hundreds of other workers who are daily alienated by norms and values which impede their healthy productivity, or whose creativity and imagination is constrained or suppressed by a culture which is outmoded and divisive. The way we do things round here is about the way we choose to allow managers to practise their craft. Often, the only induction into the managerial role has come from previous role models, for good or ill. We were recently approached by a bright young marketing executive, about to be given her first performance appraisal, with the question: 'Should I tell the truth? I know that in theory it is a good way to behave, but I have observed that those that have, in the past, have been ill used by my boss. What am I supposed to do?' Imagine, if you will, the implication of that cultural norm throughout a business of some 300 people. We could list examples of these aberrations until we were exhausted. Throughout UK enterprises we find these abominations and distortions.

Changing the way managers behave and making it stick is the omphalos of transformation. Visions, mission statements and values are necessary but not sufficient without the specification of management practices. We have offered many choices in Chapter Seven, and the task of choosing must be for the driving alliance. However, once chosen, making them stick, first by role-modelling by the senior actors and latterly by the provision of the appropriate feedback seems to be the most arduous task. Here is the middle-order point of failure. Unless managers are helped to understand the need for their behaviour to change and are provided with regular and accurate feedback about their successes and failures, no culture change will really occur. We may engage in some symbolic activity. One of Sir Colin Marshall's first decisions at BA was to close the senior managers' Mess. The symbolic impact was direct and highly visible, but its influence probably lasted less than a year. The real influence came as a result of specifying practices for every manager and making rewards contingent upon successfully implementing behaviour change. We don't believe that a culture-change activity can exist without that component being present. For us it is the *sine qua non* of culture change.

Principle Six

The devil is in the detail of the planning. Obviously the mandate and logic of the change must be widely understood and constantly repeated. The benchmark dates and events must be celebrated. The intermediate and eventual outcomes must be clear and measurable. This level of planning we take for granted. What is often less obvious is the need for alignment in the change-planning process. By alignment we mean ensuring that apparently disconnected activities or systems promote the central purpose of the change. For instance, in tackling the issues of management practices for culture change, the temptation is to see the primary-change intervention as training and subordinate feedback. Essentially, tell the management how we wish them to behave, exemplify particular values, then provide them with feedback about how they actually behave, and, hey presto, we will have culture change. In just a very few cases that may be so. More likely, however, it will be necessary to review the reward strategies and the formal performance-appraisal mechanisms which deliver the rewards. If these are not aligned to the new practices, don't be surprised if the culture change never happens. Similarly, check for alignment in the type of management-development activity that is current, also mechanisms for identification and promotion of talent in the organisation, as well as how individuals get selected for plum assignments. Unless all of these mechanisms, which are part of the way we do things around here and as such express a set of values, are made to align with the new vision, we can't expect much forward progress. So in the example we gave earlier of the performance-management process where being truthful was seen as potentially career limiting, it would be necessary to clarify the purpose of the performance-management process amongst all managers and to make very clear the sanctions for the illegitimate use of the process.

Ensuring alignment is vital, spend time reviewing (by listening) all parts of the way the business works and ensure that every part supports what you are trying to accomplish.

Similarly, with the provision of feedback. We have often been confronted by managers who have received critical feedback either about the way their team see them or from their customers and who have nowhere to turn for support, encouragement or facilitation. Our strong advice to the driving alliance would be that whenever feedback is proffered ensure that support systems are in place to guarantee that constructive action is taken immediately. In the case of attitude surveys amongst the work force, ensure that any manager heavily criticised by his/her workteam has a third-party intermediary to assist in interpreting the message and in building an action plan to fix the problems unearthed by the survey. Sometimes a competent human-resources advisor is capable of providing such assistance. Often not; lack of skill or long-standing distrust of each other, frequently makes it unlikely. If that is the case then the driving alliance, in planning the employee survey, should ensure that suitable counsellors are made available for survey interpretation and planning. Similarly, use counsellors, either internal or external, to help in the planning of action resulting from extensive customer survey data. Ensure an appropriate alignment of resources to make certain that action follows feedback.

Principle Seven

Don't let the view become the journey or spend so long in duty-free that you miss your flight. Changing your business is not a project but a process. Too often we hear senior well-intentioned people talk in terms such as 'We're doing IIP' or 'The chairman's conference will address . . .' or even 'We're doing assessment centres on all our managers', as if these individual interventions in and of themselves represent the key to major and significant business performance improvement. Surely they may make a contribution. But they are not the it of it! In the BA change plan from the start we recognised that a multiplicity of interventions would be required. Each had its own time-frame, most had to follow in a prescribed sequence, and a great many overlapped. The immediate implication of this is twofold. First, the driving alliance cannot be in absolute control at all times, nor should they be. Second, the driving alliance must be prepared to add resources to its membership. These usually come in three forms.

First, the functional specialist, frequently in human resources or marketing. Our strong advice here is that the alliance must use the professional expertise of these colleagues. However, unless the alliance maintains tight close-up involved control of the specialists often what is produced does not capture the essence of what was intended. On several occasions we have been involved with organisations where the driving alliance has handed over the production of a video or of the vision launch process to the marketing function. The results have been highly professional, but have been totally 'off-message'. Often extremely expensive, these unsatisfactory production attempts fail to capture the essence of the message and thus do more harm than good. Similarly, we would never allow most industrial relations specialists a totally free hand to design an employee profit-sharing scheme. Their level of professional sophistication often gets in the way of the need for absolute transparency in the process of calculating each individual share. Allow their advice, sign off the agreed final detail, but the overall shape is the job of the alliance, and it should not be delegated.

The second sort of additional resource comes in the form of the task force or project team. Widely used, though frequently less than totally successful, they represent very rewarding vehicles for the involvement of individuals who are identified as early champions of change. These early adopters, drawn from all levels in the organisation, can become what Australian organisations call the 'movers and shakers'. Some rules that we have found to be quite useful are:

- Ensure that the task force reports directly to the driving alliance and that the work that needs to be done is urgent.
- Define the objectives, deliverables and time scales very tightly.
- If the task force is to work on a cross-functional issue, ensure cross-functional representation.
- Insist upon early third-party facilitation.
- Guarantee access to the driving alliance at all times.
- Provide the necessary resources (time, money, office space etc.) for the group to be successful.
- Disband the group once they have delivered and ensure widespread public recognition for their efforts.

These task-force members will become the champions of the change project and some of their members may, subsequently be permanently co-opted into the driving alliance.

The third source of resource to the driving alliance is the external consultant. We believe that the essential and central role of the consultant is that of teacher, the purveyor of counsel and wisdom. Perhaps the best business consultants, however, are those that are the exception to the rule 'those that can do, those that can't teach'. For us a consultant who has worked on the same or similar real-life problems as the ones we face, has achieved some success and can act as a teacher is perhaps the perfect combination. Be wary, we suggest, of any consultancy that cannot or will not guarantee that the individuals who make the pitch will be the same individuals who do the work. The nature of many consultancy practices is that it is necessary for the bottom-line for the senior most-experienced rabbi to be on-the-road, making sales, while the work is often undertaken by lowly paid, very inexperienced 22 year olds who have just graduated from 'a good university'. The real issue for the driving alliance is to avoid developing a tactical dependency upon consultancy help, while at the same time avoiding strategic isolation. Thus, never let a consultant do work that you in the driving alliance could do or could get done in-house, while at the same time insist that your consultant provide you with strategic insight that you could never get easily for yourself. Insist that they teach you, not do the work that your own people could do. The general rules of life apply in the selection of external consultants beyond that. You must like them. You must feel able to trust them. But above all we suggest that they should be in love with your business, as much or more than you. And certainly, they should be more intrigued with the issues, than they are with their fees.

Final Instructions

We shall always be grateful to a colleague, many years our senior, and much wiser than we shall ever be, who offered as a going-away gift, a poem entitled 'Final Instructions' by the Poet Laureate of the late 1960s, Cecil Day Lewis. For those of you who have persevered thus far we offer a gentle paraphrase as our final contribution to your journey.

> Luck is all we can wish you, or need wish you
> And each time you prepare to make the superhuman effort that will
>   be required to bring about the changes you desire,
> Remember these words
> Patience, joy and selflessness

(With our apologies to Cecil Day Lewis)

APPENDIX I

Companies worldwide who have used the Service Organisation Profile

Europe
Anglia Railways
British Airways, Overseas Customer
  Service
British Telecom (CCU)
British Telecom Customer
  Communications Centre
BUPA
Chevron
Compass Security
Coopers & Lybrand Deloitte
Great Western Trains Company
InterCity
Mount Vernon and Watford NHS
  Trust
Ocean Transport and Trading
Railtrack Great Western Zone
Railtrack Midland Zone
Robert McBride Ltd
ScottishPower Generation Wholesale
  Division
ScottishPower Information Systems
  Division
Shell
SRU Ltd
SWIFT, Belgium
Thames Trains
Toyota
Unilever

USA, South America and Caribbean
Aerovias de Mexico, Mexico
Aetna Life and Casualty
Arthur D Little, Technical Research
Chevron, San Francisco
Colonial Life Insurance Company,
  Barbados
Columbia University Business School
Discover Card Services
Hoffman La Roche Inc
Johnson & Johnson Hospital Services
New Hampshire Insurance Company
Pacific Gas and Electric
Rockefeller Group
  Telecommunications Inc
Star Enterprises
Thomson Information/Publishing
  Group

Australia
Australian Airlines
Australian Resorts
Australian Telecom – Queensland
  Country Region
Email Ltd (Major Appliance Group)
National Jet Systems
Public Transport Corporation of
  Victoria
Qantas
Queensland Regional Education
  Executive
TAFE–TEQ
Wallace Bishop Jewellers

Asia Pacific
Holiday Inns

Africa
Gilbeys Distillers and Vintners, South
  Africa

APPENDIX II

Statistical data on the Service Organisation Profile		
Factor	Cronbach alpha coefficient	Split half reliability
Leadership	0.91	0.93
Customer-service mission	0.88	0.90
Adaptive culture	0.87	0.90
Management practices	0.97	0.98
Group climate	0.89	0.91
Group tension	0.82	0.87
Job satisfaction	0.88	0.89
Role overload	0.82	0.86
Role ambiguity	0.75	0.75
Career development	0.82	0.86*
* estimated		

APPENDIX III

Full matrix of factor correlations from the Service Organisation Profile

	Leadership	Mission	Culture	Management practices	Climate	Tension	Job satisfaction	Role overload	Role ambiguity	Career development
Leadership	1.00									
Service mission	0.75	1.00								
Adaptive culture	0.85	0.75	1.00							
Management practices	0.51	0.37	0.51	1.00						
Group climate	0.31	0.28	0.31	0.41	1.00					
Group tension	0.60	0.43	0.60	0.63	0.49	1.00				
Job satisfaction	0.52	0.35	0.47	0.43	0.30	0.58	1.00			
Role overload	−0.28	−0.21	−0.33	−0.28	−0.14	−0.47	−0.18	1.00		
Role ambiguity	−0.40	−0.32	−0.41	−0.48	−0.37	−0.43	−0.38	−0.23	1.00	
Career development	0.56	0.38	0.54	0.47	0.25	0.47	0.51	−0.18	−0.40	1.00

Matrix of Pearson product moment correlations of all ten factors on the Service Organisation Profile.
Sample size 16383. Missing data by mean substitution. All correlations significant beyond 0.01% level of probability.

BIBLIOGRAPHY

Allen R F & Pilnick S (1973). Confronting the shadow organisation: how to detect and defeat negative norms. *Organisational Dynamics*, Vol 1.

Bartlett C A & Ghoshal S (1994). Changing the role of top management: beyond strategy to purpose. *Harvard Business Review*, November/December

Bass B M & Stogdill R M (1990). *Handbook of Leadership*. New York: Free Press.

Belasco J A (1990). *Teaching the Elephant to Dance*. London: Hutchinson Business Books.

Bennis W D (1959). Leadership theory and administrative behaviour: the problem of authority. *Administrative Science Quarterly*, Vol IV, 259–307

Bennis W & Nanus B (1985). *Leaders – The Strategies for Taking Charge*. New York: Harper and Row.

Bernardin H J & Alvares K (1976). The managerial grid as a predictor of conflict resolution and managerial effectiveness. *Administrative Science Quarterly*, 21: 84.

Bion W R (1961). *Experiences in Groups*. New York: Basic Books.

Blake R R & Mouton J J (1976). *The New Managerial Grid*. Houston, Tx: Gulf.

Blanchard K & Johnson S (1982). *The One Minute Manager*. New York: Morrow.

Block P (1987). *The Empowered Manager*. New York: Jossey-Bass.

Boulding K (1985). *Human Betterment*. Beverly Hills, CA: Sage.

Boyatzis R E (1982). *The Competent Manager*. Chichester: Wiley.

Burke W W (1987). *Organization Development*. Reading, MA: Addison-Wesley.

Burke W W & Litwin G H (1989). *A Causal Model of Organizational Performance*. Annual Handbook for Facilitators. San Diego, CA: University Associates.

Burke W W & Litwin G H (1992). A causal model of organizational performance and change. *Journal of Management*, Vol 18 No. 3

Burns J M (1978). *Leadership*. New York: Harper and Row.

Conger J A (1991). Inspiring others; the language of leadership. *Academy of Management Executive*, Vol 5.

Douglas M (1982). *Cultural Bias*. In Douglas M (Ed) *In the Active Voice*. London: Routledge & Kegan Paul.

Egan G (1994). *Working the Shadowside*. San Francisco, CA: Jossey-Bass.

Emery F E & Trist E L (1965). The causal texture of the organizational environment. *Human Relations*, Vol 18, 21–32.

Fayol H (1949). *General and Industrial Management*. London: Pitman.

Fiedler F E (1967). *A Theory of Leadership Effectiveness*. New York: McGraw-Hill.

Fleishman E A (1953). Leadership climate, human relations training and supervisory behaviour. *Personnel Psychology*, Vol 6, 205–222.

Galtung J (1967). *Theory and Methods of Social Research*. London: George Allen and Unwin.

Gardner J W (1984). *Excellence*. New York: W W Norton, 101–102.

Goodstein L D & Burke W W (1991). Creating successful organizational change. *Organizational Dynamics*, Spring.

Hamel G & Prahalad C K (1994). *Competing for the Future*. Boston, MA: Harvard Business School Press.

Hampden-Turner C (1990). *Corporate Culture for Competitive Edge*. London: Economist Publications.

Hemphill J K (1950). *The Leader Behavior Description*. Columbus, OH: Ohio State University Press.

Hersey P & Blanchard K H (1972). Management and Organizational Behavior (2nd Edition). Englewood Cliffs, NJ: Prentice Hall.

Heskett J L, Jones T O, Loveman G W, Sasser W E Schlesinger L A (1994). Putting the service–profit chain to work. *Harvard Business Review*, March–April 164–174.

House R J (1971). A path–goal theory of leadership effectiveness. *Administrative Science Quarterly*, Vol 16, September, 321–338.

Jehn K and Shah P P (1997). *Journal of Personality and Social Psychology*. In press.

Johst H (1933). *Schlageter* Act 1 Scene 1.

Kahn R L & Katz D (1960). Leadership practices in relation to productivity and morale. In Cartwright D & Zander A (eds) *Group Dynamics Research and Theory*. London: Tavistock Publications.

Kaplan R S & Norton D P (1992). The balanced scorecard – measures that drive performance. *Harvard Business Review*, January–February.

Kaplan R S & Norton D P (1993). Putting the balanced scorecard to work. *Harvard Business Review*, January–February.

Kilman R H, Saxton M J, Sherpa R et al (1988). *Gaining Control of the Corporate Culture*. San Francisco, CA: Jossey-Bass.

Kotter J P (1990). *A Force for Change: How Leaders Differ from Management*. New York: Free Press.

Kotter J P (1992). What Leaders Really Do. *Harvard Business Review*, May–June.

Kotter J P (1995). Leading change: why transformation efforts fail. *Harvard Business Review*, March–April.

Kotter J P (1996). *Leading Change*. Boston, MA: Harvard Business School Press.

Kotter J P & Heskett J L (1992). *Corporate Culture and Performance*. New York: Free Press.

Kotter J P & Leahey J (1990). *Changing the Culture at British Airways*. Harvard Business School: Case No. 9-491-009

Litwin G, Bray J & Brooke K L (1996). *Mobilizing the Organization*. Hemel Hempstead: Prentice Hall.

Lombardo M & McCauley C (1988). *The Dynamics of Management Derailment*. Center for Creative Leadership, NC: Technical Report No. 34.

Luthans F (1988). Successful vs Effective Real Managers. *Academy of Management Executive*, Vol 2, 127–132

McCall M W et al (1978). *Studies of Managerial Work: Results and Methods*. Center for Creative Leadership, NC: Technical Report No. 9.

McCall M W & Lombardo M M (1983). What makes a top executive? *Psychology Today*, February.

McCall M W (1993). *Developing Leadership: A Look Ahead*. Center for Creative Leadership, NC.

Mintzberg H (1973). *The Nature of Managerial Work*. New York: Harper & Row.

Morgan G (1986). *Images of Organization*. London: Sage.

Morrison A, White R & Van Velsor E (1987). *Breaking the Glass Ceiling*. Reading, MA: Addison-Wesley.

Nadler D A & Tushman M L (1977). A diagnostic model for organization behavior. In *Perspectives on Behavior in Organizations* edited by Hackman J R, Lawler E E and Porter L W. New York: McGraw Hill.

Nanus B (1989). *The Leaders Edge*. Chicago, IL: Contemporary Books.

Nanus B (1992). *Visionary Leadership*. San Francisco, CA: Jossey-Bass.

Pagonis W P (1992). The work of the leader. *Harvard Business Review*, Nov–Dec.

Pascale R T & Athos A G (1981). *The Art of Japanese Management: Applications for American Executives*. New York: Warner Books.

Pauchant T C et al (1995). *In Search of Meaning*. San Francisco, CA: Jossey-Bass.

Pearce J A & David F (1987). Corporate mission statements: the bottom line. *Academy of Management Executive*, Vol 1, No 2.

Peters T & Waterman R (1982). *In Search of Excellence*. London: Harper & Row.

Presidential Commission Report on the Space Shuttle Challenger Accident. July 1986 Vol. 1, 40 and 82.

Reichheld F F & Sasser W E (1990). Zero defections: quality comes to service. *Harvard Business Review*, Sept/Oct.

Roethlisberger F J & Dickson W J (1939). *Management and the Worker*. Harvard University Press.

Ryan K D & Oestreich D K (1991). *Driving Fear out of the Workplace*. San Francisco, CA: Jossey-Bass.

Savage G T, Nix T W, Whitehead C J & Blair J D (1991). Strategies for assessing and managing organizational stakeholders. *Academy of Management Executive*, Vol 9, No. 2.

Schein E (1985). *Organizational Culture and Leadership*. San Francisco, CA: Jossey-Bass.

Schneider B & Bowen D (1985). Employee and customer perceptions of service in banks: replication and extension. *Journal of Applied Psychology*, 70, 423–433

Smircich L (1983). Concepts of culture and organizational analysis. *Administrative Science Quarterly*, 28, 339–358.

Stogdill R (1974). *Handbook of Leadership*. New York: Free Press.

Stryker P (1958). On the meaning of executive qualities. *Fortune*, 57.

Trompenaars F (1993). *Riding the Waves of Culture. Understanding Cultural Diversity in Business*. London: Nicholas Brealey.

Van Velsor E and Leslie J B (1995). Why executives derail: perspectives across time and cultures. *Academy of Management Executive*, Vol 9, No. 4.

Vroom V H and Yetton P W (1973). *Leadership and Decision-Making*. University of Pittsburgh Press.

Wallach E J (1983). Individuals and Organizations: The Cultural Match. *Training and Development Journal*, Feb.

Weick K (1983). Letters to the editor. *Fortune*, October 17 P 27.

Weisbord M R (1976). Organizational diagnosis: six places to look for trouble with or without a theory. *Group and Organization Studies*, 1, 430–447

Wilhelm W (1992). Changing corporate culture – or corporate behaviour? How to change your company. *Academy of Management Executive*, Vol 6, No. 4, 72–77.

Zaleznik A (1977). Managers and leaders: are they different? *Harvard Business Review*, May–June.

Zeithaml V A, Parasuraman A and Berry L L (1990). *Delivering Quality Service*. New York: Free Press.

AUTHOR INDEX

SUBJECT INDEX

Index compiled by Geoffrey Jones